knitting pearls

ALSO BY ANN HOOD

An Italian Wife

Knitting Yarns

The Obituary Writer

The Red Thread

Comfort: A Journey Through Grief

The Knitting Circle

An Ornithologist's Guide to Life

Somewhere Off the Coast of Maine

knitting pearls

· WRITERS WRITING ABOUT KNITTING ·

Edited by Ann Hood

W. W. NORTON & COMPANY

Independent Publishers Since 1923

New York • London

For the knitters who saved me

Jen,

Louise,

Stephanie,

Mary,

Laurie,

Nancy,

Pam,

Drake,

Karen,

and Helen

contents

8 · CONTENTS

introduction

IN TRUTH, IF MY ALMA MATER WEST WARWICK HIGH
School gave out a prize for Least Likely to Knit, surely I would
have won it. A straight-A student, I met my nemesis in Home
Economics in 1970, when all the ninth graders had to take Sewing.
I'd successfully passed the Cooking section the fall before, which
involved making no-bake cookies out of peanut butter, oats, and
chocolate and serving them to the boys in the Woodshop room.
Sewing proved more challenging. It involved cutting fabric, pinning patterns, taming a sewing machine, threading needles and
bobbins. I sweated and cursed and prayed, but that wraparound
skirt did not get made. Finally, I snuck it home to my cousin who'd
received an A the year before. She made the thing in no time, and
I tried unsuccessfully to pass it off as my own work. The teacher
knew better. She tore out all the stitches, and gave me my first B. I
vowed to never pick up anything remotely crafty again.

Many years later, after the death of my five-year-old daughter
Grace in 2002, I found myself in a yarn store not far from the
Sakonnet River in Tiverton, Rhode Island, doing what I never
imagined I would do: knitting. From the time I picked up those
number 9 needles and a skein of sky blue yarn, I was hooked. I
often say I knit my way through grief, and I do believe that is the
best way to describe how I returned to a place of hope and joy in
my life.

If you are one of the many people who read *Knitting Yarns:*

Writers on Knitting, then you know the pleasure you have in store for you here. That first anthology, published in 2013, included twenty-seven of your favorite, award-winning, bestselling writers writing on my favorite topic: knitting. The idea came to me as I watched writers like me sitting in the back rows of classrooms and lecture halls knitting. I knew why I first picked up needles and yarn back in 2002; but why had they? And why does the magic of knitting elude some people? What followed were essays (and one poem) about the transformative power of knitting; knitted gifts; knitting envy; onetime knitting; anti-knitting; the history of knitting; and knitting lessons.

Fans of that book might be surprised that twenty-seven more of your favorite, award-winning, bestselling writers have written essays just as delightful and heartbreaking, joyous and funny, wise and poignant. If you haven't read the first one, after reading *Knitting Pearls*, you surely will. *Knitting Yarns* gave us patterns by designer Helen Bingham, and one pattern by contributor Taylor Polites. This time, I'm pleased to offer you wonderful patterns by some of the best knitting stores across the country. Purl Soho in New York City, Loop in Philadelphia, Churchmouse Yarns & Teas on Bainbridge Island in Washington, Hill Country Weavers in Austin, Texas, The Yarnery in Saint Paul, Minnesota, and Knit Purl in Portland, Oregon, have contributed patterns that will make you swoon.

And speaking of swooning, here's what you have to look forward to when you read *Knitting Pearls*. Like me, some of the contributors knit their way through adversity. Caroline Leavitt's first husband asked her to make him a sweater with brontosauruses on it, but as she knit the marriage began to crumble. Lily King's daughter knit a hat during their year living in Italy, which eased her homesickness. Cynthia Chinelly knits to help her escape the worry she has for her son. Melissa Coleman hoped that knitting a sweater for everyone in her family would remove the curse of divorce. An on-again, off-again knitter, Robin Romm returned to it when her mother was dying, and now knits as she waits for a baby. Back at Ithaca College in the 1970s, Bill Roorbach joined the knitting club to get over his broken heart—and to meet girls.

Knitted gifts are important to us too. In fact, it sounds like the Christmas stockings Laura Lippman's mother knits are the same pattern as the ones from Lee Woodruff's childhood. Lippman writes about the thirty-first stocking her mother knit and why it will never be hung up. Woodruff examines the life of a marriage and adulthood. The surprise arrival of a cardigan helps Jared Flood understand the importance of homemade items, while the sweater Michael Collier's mother knit for him one Christmas helped him realize something about himself. And Nick Flynn, whose grandfather was a wool merchant, recalls the sweater his mother knit for him. Debra Gwartney's family believed you kept your troubles to yourself. But writing about the red vest her grandmother knit for her, Gwartney wonders about this advice. After her mother dies, Perri Klass poignantly reclaims all the items she'd knit for her over the years. And Stewart O'Nan reminds us how knitting for a serviceman overseas might be the greatest gift of all.

The people who knit for us are heralded here. Cathi Hanaeur's mother-in-law knit her a heather blue sweater and shared her life with Hanaeur. When Samantha van Leer knit a scarf for her mother, she discovered what her Ema got from knitting her so many sweaters. Steve Almond spent the summer he was six with his grandmother, who taught him to crochet.

Yarn whisperer Clara Parkes writes a letter to all of her unfinished knitting projects. Jane Hamilton tells us why after a summer living in the Outer Hebrides in Scotland she vowed never to knit again. Ann Leary confesses how one special knitter turned her against all knitters who followed. Stephanie Mannatt Danler calls herself an unraveler, and writes about how she let go of the idea of knitting for good. Knitting through her chemotherapy and radiation would have helped, Christina Baker Kline admits. In her essay she tells us why she didn't. After Dani Shapiro put down her yarn and needles for good, she understood a new lesson about life. And with a grandmother who was an expert knitter, Jodi Picoult writes about why she never learned herself.

I believe that knitting is not just knitting. Anne Bartlett gives us twelve lessons proving that. Maile Meloy discusses knitting as negative and positive probability, and writes about how different knitting and writing are. And Diana Gabaldon tells us how quitting the 4-H Club led to the knitting success that comes from the Starz television series of her *Outlander* novels.

What you have here, dear readers and knitters, is a stellar lineup of knitting stores and knitting essays. Kick off your shoes, curl up in your favorite chair, and dive into *Knitting Pearls*.

knitting pearls

Purl Soho
459 Broome Street
New York, NY 10013
(212) 420-8796
www.purlsoho.com

CLASSIC CUFFED HAT

MATERIALS

- **Hat with pompom:** 1 (2, 2) skeins of Purl Soho's Worsted Twist or Worsted Twist Heather, 100% merino. We used all of our new colors! Look below for a list of colors.
- **Hat without pompom:** 1 (1, 1) skeins of Purl Soho's Worsted Twist or Worsted Twist Heather, 100% merino.
- A US #5, 16-inch circular needle
- A US #7, 16-inch circular needle
- A set of US #7 double pointed needles
- 4 stitch markers (one a different color from the others)
- **Optional:** A US #6 or #7 straight needle for the Long Tail Tubular Cast On
- **Optional:** Clover Pom Pom Maker in Large

Baby Size, left, from top to bottom: Paprika Red, Pink Grapefruit, Ochre Yellow, and Yellow Zest

Kid Size, center, from top to bottom: Lichen Green, Green Turquoise, Pistachio Green, and Cardamom Green

Adult Size, right, from top to bottom: Gray Fig, Green Gray, Moody Green, and Black Green

GAUGE

Body: 20 stitches x 28 rounds = 4 x 4 inches in stockinette stitch on larger needle

Ribbing: 24 stitches x 32 rounds = 4 x 4 inches in 1 x 1 rib (unstretched) on smaller needle

SIZES

Baby (Kid, Adult)

- **Finished Body Circumference:** 15 (17, 18½) inches
- **Finished Ribbing Circumference (unstretched):** 12 (13, 14) inches
- **Finished Height (not including pompom):** 9½ (11, 12¼) inches

NOTES

For this hat I used the nice and stretchy Long Tail Tubular Cast On.

If you find yourself overwhelmed or intimidated by the Long Tail Tubular Cast On, just use a regular Long Tail Cast On (or whatever elastic cast-on method you feel comfortable with). Your hat will be just as classic and functional! If you do use a regular Long Tail Cast On, join to work in the round and proceed directly from the Ribbing section of the pattern.

PATTERN

NOTE: This pattern is also available as a printer-friendly PDF.

Begin

With the straight needle (or the larger circular needles, if you wish), use a Tubular Cast On to cast on 72 (80, 88) stitches. The first stitch you cast on, after the beginning slipknot, should be a purl stitch. Turn the work and do not join.

With the same needle, work two Foundation Rows, as explained in our Long Tail Tubular Cast On Tutorial:

Row 1: *K1 through the back loop, slip 1 with yarn in front, repeat from * to end of row. Turn.

Row 2: *K1, slip 1 with yarn in front, repeat from * to end of row. Do not turn.

Rib the Cuff

Using the smaller circular needles, place a marker and join to work in the round, being careful to not twist the stitches.

Round 1: *K1, p1, repeat from * to end of round.

Repeat Round 1 until piece measures 3 (3½, 4) inches from cast-on edge.

Work the Body

Continuing with larger circular needles, work in stockinette stitch (knit every stitch) until piece measures 8 (8¾, 9¾) from cast-on edge.

Shape the Crown

NOTE: Change to double-pointed needles when necessary.

Round 1: [k1, ssk, k13 (15, 17), k2tog, place a marker that is a different color than the end-of-round marker] three times, k1, ssk, k13 (15, 17), k2tog. [64 (72, 80) stitches]

Round 2: Knit.

Round 3: [K1, ssk, knit to 2 stitches before marker, k2tog, slip marker] four times. [8 stitches decreased]

Repeat Rounds 2 and 3 until 16 (16, 16) stitches remain.

Final Round: [K2tog] 8 times. [8 (8, 8) stitches]

Finish

Cut yarn, leaving an 8-inch tail. Thread the tail onto a tapestry needle, sew it through the remaining stitches, and pull tight. Bring the tail to the inside of the hat and weave it in. Weave in any remaining ends.

Pom Pom

Using the Medium (Large, Large) pompom maker, follow the manufacturer's instructions to make 1 pompom. Use sharp scissors to trim the pompom to 2 (2½, 3) inches diameter. Attach securely at crown. Here's how . . .

You should have 2 long tails coming from the pompom. Thread 1 tail through a tapestry needle. Insert the tapestry needle through the very top of the hat, directly to one side of the closure at the crown. Pull the tail through to the inside. Repeat with the other tail, this time inserting the needle on the opposite side of the closure at the crown. Turn the hat inside out. Firmly tie the two tails together in a tight double knot. Thread both tails onto the tapestry needle and bring the needle through the crown and up through the center of the pompom. Trim the tails to the same length as the rest of the pompom.

Now enjoy your Classic Cuffed Hat!

clothes for the living

STEVE ALMOND

*How a revelation of death when he was only six led the
author into a brief obsessive love affair with crocheting.*

W HEN I WAS SIX YEARS OLD, I SUFFERED A REVE-
lation of death. I was wandering through a grove of
pine trees near a lovely lake in the Adirondacks. I
have no idea what I was doing in that grove. In my cloying recon-
struction of the memory I'd been coaxed there by some exalted
desire to divine the truth about life, which is almost certainly bullshit. The trees probably weren't even pines.

I do remember the moment itself. Sun lancing through the
trees, the pungency of sap, then: a jabbing panic. My thinking
went like so: *At some point my heart will stop beating. Everything will
go black. I will no longer exist. That will be that.* I sobbed hysterically.

This episode marked the beginning of my brief obsessive love
affair with crochet.

I WAS IN the Adirondacks at age six because my parents had sent
me and my twin brother Mike across the country—unaccompa-
nied, on an airplane—for a visit with our maternal grandparents.

Irving and Ann Rosenthal had grown up on the Lower East Side of New York City and come of age during the Great Depression. Because of what they saw, they came to believe that the bounty of the earth should be divided more or less equally among its inhabitants.

This was a dangerous view to hold during the 1950s and Annie, who was the assistant principal of P.S. 113 in Harlem, was eventually asked to testify before the New York City Board of Education. This was all part of the work done by the House Committee on Un-American Affairs. Annie didn't testify. She took an early retirement instead. She was lucky, compared to a lot of other folks.

I knew none of this at age six. My grandparents were simply grandparents: loving, indulgent beings. They set up a little room for us in the cottage they rented on the banks of Lake Lucerne, where they came each summer to escape the sweltering Bronx. They took us swimming every day. Irving bought us fishing poles and we pulled sunfish from the brown water. They glittered like giant dimes.

It was in some ways an idyll. At least until I suffered this anxiety attack, which was no doubt triggered by the separation from our parents but was also (as I see it now) a reasonable, if precocious, reaction to the horrifying nullity of death.

MY GRANDPARENTS DID everything they could to comfort me. Nothing stuck until my grandmother presented me with a crochet needle. It was brushed aluminum, a light green model that gleamed. I fell in love with it instantly.

I'm not sure why Annie settled on a crochet needle. Perhaps I'd shown an interest in her knitting. Perhaps she'd realized, based on my thumb sucking and fingernail gnawing, that I needed something to engage my hands and thereby tame my nerves.

Whatever it was, I took to crochet with a fanatic devotion. I loved the feel of the needle in my hand, the slack sliding over my index finger, the tiny digital ballet by which the yarn slipped under the hook and the stitch was pulled snug. I loved the terminology: slipknot, magic ring, chain stitch. I loved the numbing repetition of the ritual, the idea that you could create something without thinking about it at all.

SOMETIMES, I WOULD gaze down at the yarn looping around the end of the needle and the knot slipping free and I would see the hook as a tiny little head that was being hanged and rescued over and over.

THIS WAS ALSO the summer my grandmother's brother Sam died, her favorite. She told us nothing about this, though one night Mike snuck into the kitchen after hours and caught her weeping in front of the kitchen sink. He returned to our room shaken. I was shaken, too.

We tell ourselves children don't understand death. I happen to believe just the opposite. Children see every loss as a kind of death. They experience fear and sadness as pure sensation. They are at play amid the vast graveyard of human feeling.

ANNIE SPENT A LOT of time roasting chickens and baking cookies and ironing on a battered card table. She also knit with me every day. She showed me a few of the more sophisticated stitches—it took me days to master the half-double—while my brother and grandfather played a single endless game of checkers. I worked that green needle in a silent fury, crafting nothing of consequence. I certainly don't remember finishing any particular project. I simply sat for hours with my grandmother as dusk fell around us.

She finished things: blankets and mittens and hats and ponchos and sweaters, a significant portion of the clothing I wore as a kid. As late as college I donned her cardigan sweaters. They were coveted garments among my slovenly cohort, lent out to friends and inevitably misshapen by use, the knots loosened by the idiot capering of youth until the sleeves hung down over our hands.

I REMEMBER A summer storm rolling in and releasing spindles of lightning onto the lake as I sat on a stone wall crocheting. "Put that thing away," my grandfather hollered down from the door of the cabin. "You'll wind up electrified."

I pretended to put it away but kept right on with my work after he'd gone back inside.

Years later I'd remember this exact moment, reading *The Bell Jar*:

> *It was a queer, sultry summer, the summer they electrocuted the Rosenbergs, and I didn't know what I was doing in New York . . . It had nothing to do with me, but I couldn't help wondering what it would be like, being burned alive all along your nerves.*

BY THEN, I KNEW something about the secret life my grandparents had led, how haunted they'd been by the execution of Ethel and Julius Rosenberg. As members of the Communist Party, they'd known Ethel a little bit, through friends of friends. That nice woman. That poor woman.

It was one thing to write articles under a nom de plume, or to be called before a committee. But to be executed—that was something else. It cast a pall.

Maybe I picked up on some of this anguish, too, as kids often do. In any case, I came to see knitting as some curious admixture: a therapeutic ritual that was bound up in death.

THE LITERATURE WILL back me on this. Penelope, who weaves a great shroud at her loom day after day, only to unravel her work each evening. She is trying to keep her husband Odysseus alive. Or Madame Defarge, that creature of vengeance, who knits her own sort of shroud: a record of all those the revolution will murder. Even Charlotte—wise, true friend, noble spider—spins her webs to spare Wilbur the ax. And she does save him, too. But she also dies in the end.

I'M STILL TERRIFIED of death. Some nights, when all the little people in my house have been taken under by sleep, I lie awake and face the cold truth of it. We are here like comets, flesh and chaotic feeling. Then we are gone. Boil off all the romance and myth and what's left? Exile. Disappearance. Loss.

I HAVE COME to understand this fear as arising from a failure to love.

I STILL CANNOT see a needle crochet without feeling the stab of that summer, which was its own variety of exile I guess.

It's an odd sensation: a lump of sorrow that is somehow also nostalgic. I feel an intense desire to be back there again, in the Adirondacks, in that musty cabin near Lake Lucerne, with my grandmother and her raspy laugh, with her needles knit together under the yellow lamp like tiny axes whet and whet. She didn't make shrouds. She made clothes for the living while my grandpa leaned over the checkerboard with his beautiful crooked teeth.

They were burdened people contented by simple pleasures. I should have kissed each of them more than I did. We waste so much of our hearts. Only the dying keep a full account. In their moment of passing the exact amount is revealed on our tongues, which turn black with regret.

knitting took me halfway round the world

ANNE BARTLETT

*The author gives us twelve lessons on knitting,
writing, and life.*

K NITTING TOOK ME HALFWAY ROUND THE WORLD.
Knitting and writing have much in common. Knitting taught me a great deal about writing, and writing
taught me about knitting.

But let's begin at the beginning . . .

WHEN I WAS five my mother taught me to knit garter stitch with
nice thick orange wool, and when I was six I graduated to stocking
stitch with some pillar-box red. There was only a brief lesson in
stocking stitch before she left me for the weekend with an elderly
friend. The friend had been a nurse in the First World War and she
knew everything.

I took out my knitting, but I couldn't remember how to do
purl. I knew what stocking stitch should look like and that it was
a step up from garter stitch. I wanted the kudos. I knew that for

stocking stitch you had to do alternate purl and plain, but I didn't know the word *row*. I went to my mother's friend.

I want to do one purl one plain, I said.

Like this, she said, showing me rib stitch. *One purl one plain.*

That's not right, I said. *It's not like that. It's one purl one plain.*

It IS right, she said. *THIS is IT. It's the ONLY way to do it. One purl one plain. RIB stitch.*

Language. Words. Frustration. I didn't know the words for *row* or *stocking stitch*. I knew what I wanted, but not how to get it.

LESSON 1. *You need the right words to communicate about anything.*

When I was ten my mother decided my method needed adjusting. I'd held my hand above the right hand needle, taking it off for every stitch, but now she deemed me ready to knit with the hand under the needle and minimal movement of my pointer to wrap the yarn. We were doing the good old English method, which is slower than the European, but who dares interfere with generations of mother to daughter instruction?

I tried. I protested. Awkward. My hands hurt. Too slow. My knit stitches were suddenly too tight, increased in number and the fabric developed holes. Furthermore, now I was knitting cotton. No stretch, not kind to a child's hands.

I took it to school. My friends asked what it was. *A dishcloth,* I said proudly. But a dishcloth had no traction in that circle. Dishcloths were gray and smelly, and lived in the sink, and this one, still on the needles, was gray and smelly already. Maybe it had something to do with knitting in 100°F heat.

I learned to cast off with a sense of relief. Now I could start something new.

LESSON 2. *Don't knit with yarn or patterns you don't like. Don't write things you don't like either.*

Next came the *scarf.* Baby wool on medium-sized needles, not ideal. Maybe that was all Mum had in her stash, and she was a thrifty woman. Stocking stitch alternating with slabs of a simple holey lace stitch. *Scarf* beat the hell out of *dishcloth* for status. And even my ten-year-old eyes could see that the new method had greatly improved my tension. The scarf grew.

That same year I did a massive school project, with my excited mother leaning over my shoulder. It was on her birth country, South Africa, and she had a lot of fun. It was larger and longer than any other project in the class and I felt completely overwhelmed by the great piles of resources. I hated doing it, but it won first prize.

Another writing experience from that era. My father offered me five pounds to keep a daily diary for a whole year. I only managed it for eight months, so didn't qualify for the five quid, but to my surprise I had written a book.

LESSON 3. *Stick at it. Small amounts are cumulative.*

At fifteen there was the lemon mohair jumper. That's *sweater* for you North Americans, a word I've never understood. Do Americans like to sweat? Yes, Australians like to jump! ;-) At fifteen I was an ungainly shape, and so was the jumper, but body and jumper didn't match. Sigh. I gave up knitting until my first pregnancy.

LESSON 4. *You can't undo mohair. Some things are just duds. Recycle. There are always worms as a last resort, and they love munching on stories.*

Baby clothes! My first proper knitting pattern, bought with due ceremony. I made one item and it took the whole pregnancy, a tiny blue jumper in the hope of a boy, with a cable down the middle front, flanked by two blocks of garter stitch. I reknitted that baby blue nylon many times, and finished it just in time. But the boy came out bigger than the jumper. I squeezed it over his head just once and that was it. By the end of his first week he had grown out of it. Forty years later I've still got it. I should stuff it and put it in a glass case.

LESSON 5. *Make it big. The child will grow. The same with writing; put it all down. You can edit later when you know what it's about.*

I loved having three boys, but during the fourth pregnancy, for the first time, I knitted girl clothes—one pair of white bootees, complete with embroidered pink rosebuds, and one little pink jacket. (We didn't have detailed scans back then.) When she was born I went overboard. That poor child wore nothing but pink until she was about seven. In her teens she had a love affair with brown and khaki green. Served me right.

During those years I was also part of an Australia-wide team of editorial associates working on a magazine. We met face to face every second year, but in between we had telephone hookups. So much rich discussion! My writing was enhanced as we read, discussed and planned together.

LESSON 6. *It's easy to get into a rut. Community input enhances creativity.*

More jumpers, more confidence, more experimenting. Four children under eight, a student husband, and the need to earn some cash. I searched the jobs columns, looking for the impossible job, the one I could do at home when the children were asleep. An offer of freelance editing. And joy! I found an ad for knitters. The application was a knitted swatch. I posted it with trepidation, but I passed, and along came a designer with bags of beautiful wool. Long winter evenings, with sleeping children, industriously knitting complicated intarsia patterns that sold in major designer outlets for more money than we were getting for two weeks' pay. One memorable design included a pair of legs in fishnet stockings and red high heels. I earned seventy cents an hour.

LESSON 7. *Completing big challenges gives a sense of accomplishment, but word for stitch, writing pays better.*

Number two son and I knitted squares. We sewed them all together into a jumper and added a few beads, bells and whistles. It suited his spiky hair and his sense of fun. When that boy grew up he made a pair of football bootees for his friend's first child, and taught his wife how to crochet.

When number three son was ten, he wanted a "piano jumper." I'd never designed anything. In consultation with him I knitted a vertical off-centre piano keyboard down the front, and on the back I graphed up an intarsia pattern of the first few bars of Scott Joplin's 1902 ragtime *The Entertainer*, his favorite music, made famous in 1973 by the Oscar-winning movie *The Sting*. It was a grand success and he wore it until it was too short every which way.

I edited a book about former cannibals.

LESSON 8. *Try anything. Some of the tries will work. And use good-quality materials for epic jobs—the black dye leaked into the white. If you're writing, give yourself the benefit of a quality environment. (Libraries and coffee shops!)*

One day my father, aged seventy-two, came with my mother to the city to see the cardiologist. As we lived close by I picked them up after the appointment and brought them home to our place for lunch. Dad would have surgery in a week or two. During lunch my sister-in-law rang to get the news, but while my father was speaking to her he collapsed. Our son, aged fifteen and trained by St. John, began CPR with a doctor friend who "just happened" to be in the house, but to no avail. Afterwards the doctor commended our son for his cool head and good CPR technique. Some months later my mother gave our son a jumper she had hand-spun and knitted for my father. Our son wore it for a very long time.

LESSON 9. *Knitting is an expression of love, as is the wearing of it. Let our words, written or spoken, be life-affirming.*

After my father died life became difficult. For almost a decade we seemed to be in a long dark tunnel of many kinds of grief. In the wider family there were breakups and sad children. Number one son was seriously ill and we thought he might die. Several people we loved did die, including babies and young women. Two more friends took their own lives. Later I found myself advocating for two disturbed young men through a distressingly long, sad court case. Meanwhile our family was going through rapid transition; our own children were leaving home, leaving the country, getting married, having babies.

Some aspects of life were wonderful and others painful and

wrenching. No time to knit! One day I collapsed and ended up in an ambulance.

LESSON 10. *Sometimes words are inadequate; sometimes you can't do anything except survive. Even then, if you really want, you can probably still knit—at the wake, at the wedding, in court—or at least, if not at them, on the way home. It might just be the relaxation you need.*

Suddenly the dark tunnel ended. We moved house, my husband started a new job, our family was peaceful and settled, and we had good holidays. Over time, slowly, I left the burnout behind and re-engaged with normal life. After twenty-three years I returned to university to study creative writing, and in that protected and peaceful environment had the best fun of my life. I even did some knitting.

During a workshop our professor introduced us to the opening passage of Gertrude Stein's *Paris, France*, which begins like this:

> *I was only four years old when I was first in Paris and talked french there and was photographed there and went to school there, and ate soup for early breakfast and had leg of mutton and spinach for lunch, I always liked spinach, and a black cat jumped on my mother's back . . .*

What fun! I thought. *I'd like to have a go at that—fluid word association, loose punctuation, racy rhythms.* I had been brewing a piece about a woman throwing rose petals over a church congregation, and I made a note in my journal.

If you read too much of this [Stein] it would certainly become tedious, but as a first experience I felt bowled along like a ball in a river . . . I could try this kind of voice for the roses piece—it would suit the mad woman rather well. As my friend Ray said, Stein loops around like a clover leaf, in and out, in to the centre again. It might not work at all...But it will be fun to try, looping in and out in a large knitting pattern.

There's the word in the last sentence, *knitting*, knitting as metaphor, to describe a writing style. At the time I barely noticed it, and it was only in rereading the journal years later that I discovered that this was the very point at which I transferred from knitting as metaphor to knitting as subject matter.

LESSON 11. *The best work is preceded by play.*

As the journal clearly demonstrates, I set out to write about roses, but what came out was knitting. All my dammed-up experience of knitting erupted in a gush of writing. I wrote it fast, in a kind of a flush, and with great pleasure.

My name is Martha. I like knitting. I like the order it makes. If you go *(P1 K1) rpt all along the row, and then back again the same, it makes rib. If you have odd stitches. If you have even stitches it makes moss stitch. Rib is for ribbing, for cuffs and collars and bands on the bottom, for necklines, and maybe to make a pucker in the pattern. Puckers, evenly spaced, drawn in and stretching out, make for interest. I'm interested in knitting. I'm very interested in knitting. It interests me . . .

And so it continued, a smooth uninterrupted flow, a total surprise, for a couple of pages. And then it stopped.

I made another note in the journal.

Where did that come from? There are no roses at all. I thought I'd find out a bit about Martha, and there she is, all finished up with knitting. But that was lots of fun!!

What to do with it? Such an odd little piece, not much use for anything. I filed it away. I didn't forget it, because the writing experience had been exhilarating, but it didn't seem to fit anywhere.

Time passed. I finished the course. I had time to knit again and during the next two years wrote commissioned nonfiction. When I was nearing the end, a friend, one of my former tutors, persuaded me to apply for a creative writing PhD at the University of Adelaide. I was even offered a scholarship. Paid writing time in a supportive environment? Impossible to resist.

Early in the first year I was required to read from the work in progress, but the work was not progressing very well, so I read the knitting piece instead. I thought it had too many technical terms to appeal to an academic and potentially non-knitting audience, but it was warmly received. There was lavish encouragement to explore this character further.

And so the novel *Knitting* began, though of course I didn't know it then—it was simply an extended experiment that just might become something larger. Along the way I researched knitting in many forms—actual knitting like the blue silk vest Charles I wore when he was beheaded; knitting as a plot device as per Marelle Day's *Lambs of God* or Elizabeth Stead's *Knitting Emily Bridget*; knitting as history as in Bishop Richard Rutt's superb work, *The History of Knitting*; knitting as art form in various exhibitions; and finally, knitting as metaphor for unity and healing, as it became in my own work. I knitted as I wrote, to keep the writing grounded: concurrently with the novel I produced two jumpers, two pairs of socks and half a scarf.

After the decade of grief, knitting was healing, and so was writing about it. It's hardly surprising that the two main characters, one a bossy academic consumed with grief, the other an unboundaried fragile artist, began to represent opposite extremes of my personality. In the novel these two very different women, one a wordsmith and one a knitter, work painfully towards a retrospective exhibition of knitted garments. In the process they both offer and receive healing—albeit with the help of a third party.

As for the rest, it's a long story with a touch of the miraculous, but eventually the novel was published in America, Australia and the United Kingdom. And that's how knitting took me halfway round the world.

Lesson 12: *Don't give up. Somebody out there is on your side.*

unraveling

CYNTHIA CHINELLY

*Knitting keeps the author from thinking of her troubled son
and opens up a path to memories.*

YOU SIT IN THE KITCHEN, WINDOWS OPEN, THE FAMIL-
iar blue half-light of dawn slipping in. You try hard to
think of anything but him. There is the harsh squawk of
the yellow-crowned night heron, returning after a night of forag-
ing. There is the rustle of an ovenbird in the leafy understory of a
palm. You imagine her nest, an adobe cup, perfect and safe. And
there, at the edge of the white mangroves, a green heron hunches
on slender legs, waiting.

The clock in your heart thrums and you do not think of him,
the boy who dreamed all dreams, the son whose sadness now is
large and deep.

So you sit and open what seems like a present, a gift as light as
a breath, the turns of tissue paper revealing a luster of silk yarn,
the color of a dove or a star or a prayer candle. You drape the
loop of yarn around the edge of the table and start by forming a
butterfly, a figure-8 pattern around your thumb and index finger,
winding until the wraps have reached some bulk. Then bringing
up the wings of silk, as you have been taught, you try to blink

away the shadowbox hung in his childhood room: monarch, giant swallowtail, painted lady, Florida leafwing. The wisp of his net high in the hot sky of a summer afternoon, his face soft to every possible hope.

You begin to wind.

You are careful to keep the tension of the yarn loose. Neatness isn't important when rolling a ball of yarn. Looseness is. It's okay, even helpful, to let the yarn overlap your fingers slightly. You wrap, slowly rotating the ball counterclockwise. Counterclockwise. Leftward. Backward. Away. In reverse. Earthward. Homeward. To the place before his addiction. To the place before the blackouts, before the thin glaze of white powder on fingers and lips, before the daily litany of small deaths in the bedroom, in the yard, in parking lots, behind storefronts. To the place where this radiant boy sat in the backseat of the car caught up in the sweet rhythm of a cross-country trip, planning stops around roadside attractions: Gatorama, the Corn Palace, Wigwam Village, the Pez Museum. You still remember whole years of infinite possibilities, of a boy's voice so ripe with light that your heart was swept clean.

The ball of yarn is getting bigger, more spherical, and it is still surprising to you that this will ever be anything else. A pristine wedding shawl for after the ceremony, after the drinking, the dancing, as a late May night cools down and morning breaks into a happy weariness. An ethereal scarf, cotton and silk, beside a bed in a rented duplex in a small college town. Summer socks—small wisps alight on a rocker. But today you decide on a cowl, unnecessary, really, in this place where you live, where the swish of ocean breezes, no matter how manic, are still warm. But you are convinced the cloud-like scarf will dull the tick tick tick of the pulse in the hollow of your throat, a too-visible history under the weight of memory.

When you were fourteen and living in upstate New York, so far away from Florida and sorrow, your mom gave you two shiny pink knitting needles and a few dollars to buy yarn at Woolworth's. You took a boy, a couple of years older, on the walk. The yarn then, no more than an excuse to stop behind the shopping plaza and feel the restless heat of hands and lips. And breath. And you didn't mind the love bites he left on your neck, constant reminders that turned over in your heart those simple afternoons. And he followed you into Woolworth's and helped you pick out the soft green yarn because, yes, he would love a scarf and he would wear it all winter, tied closely around his neck against the icy winds of Lake Ontario. So you learned to knit because of love or something close to it. Green stitches gathering one by one until you saw before you what you had imagined.

The sun is up now, but it is still early and you know you have some time before the chores and the traffic and the job. With the silk rolled, you pull out two cones of slub cotton, undyed, the main yarn for the cowl. You begin to cast on. A slipknot. A foundation. A beginning. You once read, "Knowing how to tie a slipknot could save your life." Could it save his life? This running knot? This knot you used to tame your tents against the cozy rains of cross-country trips? There was St. Mary's, Georgia, and the campsite near the tidal river. His small hands were a bit wobbly as he tied the fishing line—the twist, the loop, and then the slip. A neat, strong, durable knot. A knot to cast his hopes on. And yours. There was the Rio Grande River, the knotted rope securing mom and dad and son against rapids that broke in every direction. How terrified you were that you would all be swept away, disappearing over the falls, and how you had made such a bad decision, until you saw his face and a smile so large it drank up all that fear.

A slipknot, so easily undone. Just pull one of the ends. Watch as it unravels. Watch as your son stands full-grown before you. Thin, restless, the weight of grief unhinging him until he's barely recognizable. The Camels and pills and pot. What is at his back that is too great to be forgiven? How many pasts has he lost? How terrified you are that you all will be swept away, disappearing over the falls, and how you have made so many bad decisions, to bring him to this.

A slipknot. A simple noose.

You still yourself. You learned to knit because of love or something close to it. The pattern asks for 184 stitches. So many to lose track of. You use a row counter. A click for each stitch. You need to concentrate. The yarn is called Silken Straw and is so delicate that if you cast on too tightly the silk will shred, unravel to where it will be impossible to tell where one stitch ends and another begins. Where one love ends and another begins. The boy with the green scarf ending. The boy with the blue scarf beginning. A lanky boy on the sleeping porch of his parents' home. A blistering night, a late August thunderstorm offering little relief. There was close, quiet talk of how the both of you would spend the last couple of weeks before heading off to separate schools. You sat in a rocker believing it was the heaviness of the air that made it hard to breathe.

And then the real boy, or man really, that helped you make this son. The man you set up house with, and married. This beautiful man who made this beautiful boy, out of love. The man who resurrects worlds from ink, who tries to give this son a happy ending: a ribbon of silk, unfailing.

A click for each stitch on this circular needle, a number 4, and your fingers are clumsy, never having done such fine work. You tilt the right needle to the right and insert the left needle into the loop you've pulled up. You move slowly, too slowly perhaps, unlike the thousand starlings flying through the morning light above this house. But even so, you drop the loop. You lose it. How will you get through this thing that started from love? You begin again. Insert the needle into the stitch. Pull the silk through. How careful you need to be. But being careful isn't enough. You have learned this. Mistakes are made. Some can be forgiven, over-looked. Others take root and will not let go.

You came back to knitting because of your son. You thought it would give you back that easeful life, bright from its loom. And sometimes it does. But most times the rhythm of needles is not enough and before long the mind and the heart collide, and you cannot forget the way he held your arm, white-knuckled in that white water of the Rio Grande, as if you were enough so he could open himself to that grand rush of beauty. How will you get through this?

The kitchen windows are open and the South Florida winter sun bleeds in. You try hard to think of anything but him.

casting off a spell

MELISSA COLEMAN

*The author hoped for a happy heart. Could knitting sweaters
for each member of her family break the curse divorce had put
on them?*

THE FATES MUST HAVE BEEN NATTERING ABOVE, SPIN-
ning on their eternal spindles, when I came across a
half-finished sweater I'd begun in my twenties for my
stepmother, Gerry. Running the coiled fibers through my fingers,
I remembered a sense I had, when sitting with Gerry as she tol-
erantly taught me to knit, of a pattern glimmering like a spider's
web behind the visible world—one that, if only we could see it in
its entirety, would make sense of everything. At the moment, my
marriage was in trouble and I could've used such a pattern. Why
had I abandoned this sweater?

This sweater was part of a surefire plan I'd devised years ago to
save myself from heartbreaks like the one I now faced. In the fall
of my twenty-second year, I'd just broken up with my first post-
school boyfriend, and was visiting friends who lived on Ashbury
Street, in the L House, we called it, because everyone's names
began with L, except Missy.

Missy and I were knitting on the stoop while the Deadheads

came to smoke joints on the steps of Jerry Garcia's onetime apartment next door. Our long dark hair fell forward across our shoulders as Missy's smoothly tapered fingers coaxed a scarf from her needles and I plotted a pattern on the hat in my lap, and we spoke of our struggles with romantic relationships, and as children of divorce, our pessimism about love.

"Like my college roommate used to say," I told Missy. "Never knit for a boyfriend because he'll dump you and then he'll have a sweater, but what will you have?"

"Ha," Missy replied. "I just knit for my dad. It never seems worth it to give up things for love."

Our needles click-clacked as the Deadheads came and went, and a plan began to form in my heart. It was born from a book I'd had as a child, a brightly illustrated edition of *The Six Swans* by the Brothers Grimm. In my memory it went something like this: A girl's six brothers are turned to swans by their evil stepmother. To break the curse, she has to knit them six shirts out of starflowers over the next six years and not laugh or utter a word.

While she works to complete her task, a king falls in love with her and they marry. Each time she bears him a child, the wicked stepmother secretly steals it away and finally convinces the king his wife must be burned at the stake. As she is led to her death, the swans fly down and she throws the shirts over them and they turn back into her brothers. She can now speak and tell the truth about what happened. The wicked stepmother is banished, the children are returned, and they all, of course, live happily ever after.

My heart, too, hoped to live happily ever after, so I determined I'd knit a sweater for each member of my family to break the spell I perceived divorce to have cast upon us, and to save me from a divorce of my own. One for my father, mother, first stepmother, stepdad, sister, and brother—made six. In some versions, the fairy tale featured seven swans so I figured I could include my new step-mother, but not her son. So seven sweaters—well, maybe eight, in as many years.

First came a heather gray crew neck for my father knitted that winter while living at home in Maine and dating, but ultimately losing, a childhood sweetheart. Next, there was a cranberry red J. Crew roll-neck for my second stepmom, made during the next summer in the Utah canyon lands as I let go of reconciliation with both the childhood sweetheart and the first post-school boyfriend. I was on a roll, confidently working from base to armpits on circu-lar needles—when I ran into M.

My heart did a triple cartwheel to see him strolling toward me down an aisle in the nearest grocery store, three hours from my post in the canyon lands. A few summers earlier, while volun-teering on a river, I'd secretly fallen in love with his sandy-haired, ocean-eyed good looks and skill rowing an oar-frame raft through whitewater rapids. He was tall, masculine and compelling, and the funniest storyteller I'd ever met. Now he pulled me into a hug and his more exciting world, inviting me to dinner and proposing we camp out in the desert that night.

While we waited for our food, he told me of working and liv-ing in the ranger station that my favorite environmental writer, Ed Abbey, once inhabited. I was a goner before the first drink. We laughed outrageously through the meal, then scrambled onto the red rock to set up a tent and zip our sleeping bags together against the evening cool.

When he reached over to touch my face for the first time, I felt a tenderness and surrender I hadn't known since early childhood, before my family fell apart. Of course, soon after that his radio began to chatter, calling him out on an emergency rescue, and so I was touched instead by his innate skill at helping a boy who'd fallen from a rock and dislocated his shoulder. This was why I was knitting these sweaters, I thought, as I witnessed his gentle competence with trauma. By the time I was thirty, the eight years and sweaters would be done, and I could safely marry this man.

On my next days off, I planned to join Missy and the L Gang at a bluegrass festival in Colorado. On a barren stretch of road, a few hours into the six-hour drive, my head went leaden in the heat as a white emptiness spread through my body. I stuttered awake and tried to correct the car, but not before it skidded off the road and rolled across the desert like a tumbleweed.

I called M from a remote emergency room—hair and skin layered with red sand, lacerations on my face, and a broken arm in a cast. The meds made the world clear at its root—all was either love, or pain, or this new place beyond both. When I looked up from the gurney to see M framed in the doorway, his green eyes were as calm and knowing about the mirage of pain as they'd been on the rescue.

He told me stories as he drove me home, and I laughed despite the hurt. He cleaned me up, hydrated my delirium, put me to bed, and lay beside me through the night. When I drifted awake to find he was still there, I told him he was the only person I wanted to come for me. He took me in his arms and held me with tenderness, but as soon as I felt that delicate place of surrender, a part of me began pulling away. Somewhere in the past, I'd lost the ability to feel safe in a relationship, and in myself, and he probably sensed that, and so put up his own guard.

M and I would see each other after that, but there was no more commitment than the moment, and as afraid of love as I was, I could never fully trust his intentions, or my own. Yet I held on to the hope that I just needed to finish my knitting and we could get to happily ever after.

A few years later, I'd given the red roll-neck to my second step-mom, a green roll-neck to my mother, and begun that sleeveless sweater for Gerry, made with Peace Fleece yarn spun by Russian shepherds in reconciliation from the Cold War. It called for a star pattern edging for the arms and neck that I was a little worried about, but I was again confidently working from base to armpits on circular needles, again back in the canyon lands, again a three-hour drive from M.

All I knew as I sped down the black line of tarmac toward town was that I wanted to try the safety of M's arms once more. In honor of Jerry Garcia's recent passing, I cranked "Brokedown Palace" on the car stereo, and imagined those Ashbury Street steps covered now in garlands. What I didn't know was that M had got-ten engaged. His fiancée was for him what I wished he'd be for me. Though I understood he had no knowledge of the hope I'd knitted around him, it felt as if I'd missed passage to the next stage in life.

In the crestfallen time that followed, I still toted around Gerry's Peace Fleece, but there was little chance to figure out the arm and neck edging. I took a job in Alaska for the winter (because what else does one do when heartbroken?), and after returning, started work at a magazine. Writing began to fill the time I'd once spent knit-ting, and I soon put away the half-finished project for good.

As it happened, I'd have just finished the eight sweaters and years around the time I started dating my husband, Eric. Sweaters be damned, I married him anyway. There's a temptation to think the trouble we're having is because I never broke the curse. And in another coincidence, our twin girls are now nine, the same age I was when my sister and I entered the ranks of children of divorce in the 1970s.

Part of me wonders if finishing the eight sweaters might help. Fairy tales, after all, are about personal transformation; they contain the distilled wisdom to guide you through. In my tale there were stepmothers, but not evil ones, yet I see that the struggles with my parents' divorces as a kid provided the impetus for growth that I needed. Instead of knitting, it's been the work of writing that's helped me find my voice and place in life like the girl in "The Six Swans," but there's still a piece I'm grappling with around feeling safe in relationships, and in myself.

And so this return to knitting is to that old hope of reuniting the threads of my unraveling family. I find my fingers know how to pick up the Peace Fleece yarn and keep going, even though I don't know who to ask for help with the arm edging, or who to give it to when done. Gerry, both knitting teacher and stepmother, has been gone a few years now, to a rare disease that took first her balance, then her voice, and finally her breath.

As I try to make sense of the edging, I find knitting is only about the illusion of control—if you follow this pattern, you'll get this result—but, as any knitter knows, it's never that easy. Maybe trying to control an outcome is simply an effort to avoid pain. Maybe it's better to have faith that things will unravel or knit together as they should, pain and all.

There's a sense I get that Gerry looks after me still, as she did ever since she came into my life when I was nine. We all have helpers like this. They knit with the Fates, sending little glimmering clues to that master spiderweb pattern. Her sweater is one. It restores hope, and when there's hope, there's the patience to keep knitting and writing—or searching for needles in haystacks—until you find that the love you thought you lost was right there all along.

big maroon sweater

MICHAEL COLLIER

*When the author's mother knits him a sweater to keep him
warm in college in snowy Connecticut, the gift brings him to
startling realizations about himself.*

THE FIRST TIME I SAW SNOW FALLING IN THE AIR IN big thick flakes I was twenty, standing in a T-shirt, outside the dorm of the college in Connecticut I had transferred to. It was a celestial revelation and an initiation into the necessity of owning more than a hooded sweatshirt and Levi's jacket, both of which were hanging in my closet. Until that point, I had no experience that would give me, as Wallace Stevens put it, "a mind of winter." I grew up in Phoenix, Arizona. Winters were so mild that parkas, sweatshirts, light jackets, or sweaters were adequate to keep one warm. Attesting to this was the never-worn, forever-sheathed-in-a-dry-cleaner's-bag, blue wool overcoat my father brought with him when he moved from the Midwest in 1948. It was a neglected relic of the ice and snow and slush that had pro-voked him and most of our neighbors to leave Chicago, Minneapo-lis, Madison, Columbus, Indianapolis, a few from Long Island and New Jersey, wherever those places were, and one, I recall, from Fort Mead, Maryland. I grew up inculcated with the twin ideas that no one in her right mind would live where winter existed and no one would ever voluntarily move to such a place. And yet, while hell would almost literally have to freeze over before a blizzard hit Phoenix, during the so-called winter months, my father kept a cautious eye on the weather. Just a hint from Art Brock, the KPHO television weatherman, of the possibility of frost sent my father outside with our yellow and blue checked picnic blanket to drape the windshield of his car, lest he find it bearded with ice in the morning.

The fact that I had decided all on my own to leave the Bay Area, where I had spent my first year at Santa Clara University, for a college in New England that no one in my family had ever heard of was an act of instinctual derangement on my part, like a Canada goose breaking formation to head north in a snowstorm. My parents didn't say, "You're going to freeze." No, nothing like that, which was in keeping with the silent way my family treated mystifications and disagreements. Instead, shortly after arriving at Connecticut College, I learned from my youngest sister, in a letter, that my mother was knitting me a sweater. The letter seemed to be merely informing me of a fact but what it masked, I found out later, was that my sister, as well, worried about my ability to survive a real winter, had started sewing a quilt for me. Actually, she was sewing two quilts, the other for a boyfriend who had gone off to South Bend to play football for Notre Dame.

That my mother and sister had taken up knitting and sewing on my behalf wasn't completely surprising. Although these were activities that visited the house sporadically, I wouldn't say either of them possessed the craft gene nor would I characterize their temperaments as the kind allowing them to lose themselves in work that was infinitely repetitive, requiring hours and hours devoted to a single task.

Task is the operative word. My family, in general, was not good at tasks. We were better at enthusiasms and distractions. Experts at starting things, connoisseurs of beginnings. Boredom set in quickly. Although boredom is a word I was trying to avoid because I'm aware that knitters and quilters find such work soothing and meditative, hardly work at all. In fact, I've noticed that knitters who practice their craft at a poetry reading, let's say, are so lost in the activity they are oblivious to the chopstick-like clack their needles make, offering a kind of counter-meter to the recitation. I've noticed as well that knitters can sit in an airport lounge and weave like a spider while carrying on serious people-watching. This is a chew-gum-and-walk-at-the-same-time crowd and an occupation ideal for a zombie.

This doesn't mean that we didn't try to take up tasks, and by "we," I mean my mother, four sisters, and me. Me because until I was ten my father was out on the road as a traveling salesman a significant amount of time and as a result I fell under total female supervision. If I had been a child who liked to be by himself, if loneliness had been my métier, I would have had a much looser association with the preoccupations of my supervisors, such as the seasonal attempt at dress making. This started with a visit to Landy's, the neighborhood five-and-dime, to pick out patterns offered by McCall's, Simplicity, and Butterick. My sisters walked their fingers slowly over miles of envelopes whose covers held simple line drawings of the styles the patterns would yield, if you followed the pattern correctly. I knew from attempts to make model airplanes how difficult this was and how deceptive were the instructions and how enticing the pictures on the boxes.

As my mother and sisters decided on what would determine the look of that season, I was required, when I was very young, to stick close because I had early on developed an Alzheimer's-like habit of wandering away from wherever I was supposed to be. Once, as a two-year-old, I was found by a "kind lady," a phrase my mother used, wandering in an alley a few blocks from my house. She took me inside where we sat on display in her front window and waited for a car driven very slowly by a terrified woman to appear in the street.

Thinking about these outings to the five-and-dime now, I feel fidgety and restless, the way I did then, running through me like a current. I can see that I'm holding on to the display table above me as if I'm gripping the edge of a cliff, my head looking down at my feet, my body jack-knifed as I twist and pivot. I'm desperate with impatience, tortured by the boredom. In these situations complaining and being antsy were ineffective. To get a strong, distracting response, I needed to become a nuisance. I needed to waggle my fanny until one of my sisters told me with some insistence to stay still, but that was not being a nuisance. Being a nuisance started when I opened my mouth slowly so that my lips stretched saliva into soapy, ballooning transparencies of spit bubbles. And then I would turn my head to look at my sisters and as I did I accompanied the bubbles with a bleating "maw-maw-maw" that even I myself can't bear.

After the task of picking the patterns was completed, the even more tedious activity of choosing material had to be done, which eventually included finding a clerk who would unroll the bolts of cloth and cut the appropriate yardage on a large flat table trimmed with yardsticks. Once this was accomplished, all of it was brought home in big, crinkly paper sacks that might remain unmolested in one of my sister's bedrooms for some days before my mother was prodded into setting up her sewing machine, a black Singer with gold script and scrolled filigree. Most of the time it lived in a vaguely beehive-shaped wooden box. But when the machine was in use, it stood in the middle of the living room on a table like a fetish, until the work was completed. It had a light tucked up under the thick arm, and the arm, if you turned your head sideways, had the shapeliness of a dancer's leg. The sound the motor made was a whirr but it also delivered a vibration that ran through the floor like the footsteps of a child running back and forth in a small room. My mother worked with the intensity of a machinist as she turned the Singer's balance wheel by pushing it up with her palm. A short, quick movement that got the needle placed where she wanted it, above the material, and then she pressed the foot control slowly at first and then much faster as her fingers kept the fabric flat while at the same time fed it under the reciprocating needle.

The dining room table, protected with felt pads usually brought out for Thanksgiving and Christmas dinners, was used to spread out the pattern's beige-colored sheets, stenciled with black lines and printed instructions, and which had been unfolded and flattened carefully. The energy and discipline needed to manufacture a skirt, sundress, culottes, or prom gown was manifest the moment the pattern was unwrapped and laid out on the table. The paper was thinner than a kite's or shoebox tissue, and like a road map, once it was taken out of its envelope and opened, it could never regain its original shape. And also like a road map, it was not so easy to follow, at least judging from the amount of time spent turning the sections of the pattern every which way before they were scissored into pieces. These were matched with the material and then the material was cut into roughly corresponding shapes. The cutting went fairly quickly but when it came to pinning the gossamer paper to the fabric, the operation slowed considerably. It also produced dangerous conditions in the living room as pins were apt to be dropped or roll off the table into the twisted pile of the very shaggy shag carpeting where they often landed pointed end up. Not only did the pattern have to lie smoothly over the material but it had to be arranged in such a way as to ensure the design would align across seams.

Once all of the pieces had been cut, it was then mostly up to my mother to be the seamstress and sit behind the Singer for the required hours. I don't remember her instructing my sisters in the art of sewing. I think she followed the path of least resistance, which was to do it all herself. Occasionally, one of my sisters was required to appear so that my mother could compare the waist she had made to the waist that would wear it. Adjustments were frequent, akin to revision. And sometimes things went so wrong or moved beyond my mother's skills that Mrs. Kramer, a seamstress who worked out of a hot and cheerless house a block and a half away, was brought in to finish up.

Sewing gave way to knitting when my first niece arrived. I was still in grade school. Appearing on the heels, so to speak, of her birth, as if delivered by the stork of grandmothers, was a knitting basket, more like a very small laundry hamper. It became a fixture by the side of the couch in the living room, where needles poked up through hanks of yarn, instruction booklets were folded open in uneven creases, and shards of sweaters-in-progress draped over its canvas sides. My mother knitted at moments during the day, when she could find them, but mostly I remember her sitting on the couch as dinner cooked and my father in the adjacent family room watched the news. She has a cocktail, half a jigger of scotch with a lot of ice and water. Reading glasses, hanging on a lanyard, that have slipped to the end of her nose. She's cracking chewing gum, a habit my father disapproved of but which I always thought made her seem youthful. Oh, and her legs are crossed, the top one jiggling as if she's giving a ride to the grandchild she's knitting for. Occasionally, she says "damn," and the jiggling leg stops as she picks up the dropped stitch. Or she's holding the shard up to the light as if to see the whole in the fragment or check the tightness of the knots. These are elfin-size garments you could put on any number of the dolls my sisters left behind in their closets.

While a dress could be sewn in a couple of days, a sweater grew slowly: the back, front panels, and arms accruing their forms over a brief eon. Instead of a pattern based on a paper template, knitting required the counting of stitches per row and the numbering of rows per piece. It was much more of an *ex nihilo* production. But the biggest difference, I think, was that knitting allowed my mother to concentrate in a meditative way because the activity was so thoroughly solitary. What a relief it must have been for her to be able to make something in a calm, unhurried manner which might be handed down to future arrivals and perhaps even kept as a modest heirloom or memento. Knitting as such represented futurity. Sweaters were made to grow into, while sewing of the kind she did for my sisters represented the present and the anxiety of creating an identity from the ephemeral and arbitrary rules of style and fashion.

Forty years on, I still have the sweater my mother made for me the first winter I spent in Connecticut. I have as well an Irish fisherman sweater I picked up in Wales almost as long ago. These are stored in a cedar chest along with a sweater that was given to me by Victor Prutu, in Bucharest, in March of 1977. Victor was the cousin of Luli, the Romanian flat mate I had in London where I'd been living that year and who had denounced her Romanian citizenship in order to remain in England. When I left London, I wanted to take the longest way possible back to Arizona, a route that would allow me to claim I had circled the globe. One of the legs was on the Trans-Siberian Railroad. Since Bucharest was

more or less on the way to Moscow, I made a plan with the help of
Luli to visit her mother and be a kind of emissary from her exiled
daughter. Victor and I were close in age and he spoke English. It
was incomprehensible to him that anyone would go voluntarily to
the Soviet Union and that I was crossing Siberia, albeit on a train,
constituted madness. He kept telling me I would freeze to death.
"Think *Doctor Zhivago* but without that Lara," he teased.

The night I left Bucharest, he took me to the train station and
followed me out the length of the platform to make sure I boarded
the correct car. As we exchanged the last of several friendly
embraces, he slipped off his coat and pulled the sweater he was
wearing underneath it over his head and gave it to me. "You're
going to freeze. It's certain," he said, holding it out and shaking
it at me. The sweater, a V-neck, was made of thick yarn, and was
the color of a Steller's jay, royal blue and black. The V was deep,
plunging, you might say, and had a wide, flat border, and where
the sleeves met the shoulders, the pattern of stitching changed to
form something like a band. Later, in my berth, when I tried it on,
I could see that it fell well short of my waist and that there was a
mend at the bottom of the V, but it warmed me immediately and
the way it fit snugly on my shoulders was like a pair of firm, reas-
suring hands.

I wore Victor's sweater across Siberia and then two decades
beyond, until the shrinking effects of time required me to retire
it. Someone less sentimental, less susceptible to imbuing objects
with emotional significance, might have long ago given that
sweater, and the others, to Goodwill. In fact, when I started
thinking about writing this essay, I wasn't certain if I hadn't given
them away but it took only a small amount of rooting around to
find both of them in the woolly, fragrant vault of the cedar chest,
which also preserves my navy blue Cricketeer wedding suit as

well as the Boy Scout uniform that last fit me, barely, when I was thirteen. And there are other relics: a rough wool coat inherited from the writer William Maxwell, who had inherited it from Frank O'Connor, and a vest the poet Agha Shahid Ali brought as a gift from Srinagar.

For many years, folded at the bottom of the chest, was the dark blue overcoat my father had brought from the Midwest. The one that hung in the closet of the house in Phoenix. My mother sent it to me when my wife and I moved to Washington, D.C., in 1981. I put it to hard use for twenty years, until the lining disintegrated and moths made a Milky Way of it with their star-shaped holes. Even though it was in a decrepit state, I couldn't part with it. The coat had been like Jesus' cloak. I needed only to touch it to feel a healing bond with my father. Plus, it came from a time in his life before he was married and knowing this created a sense of solidarity with his younger self, one, of course, that was wholly imagined. But shortly after my father died and my wife coincidentally was making a sensible attempt to purge us of unnecessary belongings, the coat came up for consideration. This wasn't the first time she'd held it up by its frayed collar for me to decide its fate. Unlike the wedding suit and scout uniform, which seemed like commemorative garments, items meant for an archive, my father's coat had been like a second skin, but now that he was dead, it was dead, too. It was easy, surprisingly easy, to give up.

When I came home from Connecticut for my first winter break, my sister had taken over the floor of the living room in an attempt to finish the quilts she had started weeks before. Christmas was a few days away and she had the panicked look of someone who had waited too long before beginning to study for a final exam. Squares of cloth that would serve as panels for the quilt were scattered around like oversized drink coasters. "It's for John," she said, her boyfriend, not letting on that there was a second, finished quilt rolled up like a sleeping bag in her closet.

The quilt, large enough for a double bed, had a dark brown backing on which squares of various colored cloth were sewn. A layer of white batting was fixed between, and this gave it significant R-value. Twists of brown yarn had been stitched through the quilt in random fashion to hold the three layers together. Two-legged tassels that within a few years were the first of my sister's handiwork to unravel, followed by the finer seams that joined the squares together, tears from which the batting rose up like foam.

In 1980, after breaking up with a girlfriend I'd been living with, and a stealthy decampment from her apartment, the quilt got left behind. Many years later, I ran into the person who dated the former girlfriend after I had absconded. Once we established our bona fides regarding our common relationship, he told me, among other dispiriting things, that what she referred to as "Michael's quilt" had been put to use by them on more than a few occasions as a ground cloth. This information should have wounded me more deeply than it did, especially since it had been a torture for my sister to make and also because it was warm and useful. But at the time leaving behind the quilt was a small price to pay for disentangling from an unhappy situation, even if abandoning it, as I did, was a manifestation of the cowardly way I disappeared.

The chaos generated in the living room by my sister didn't keep me from noticing the billows of yarn, like a bouquet of hydrangeas, crammed into my mother's knitting basket beside the couch. These were the trappings of the sweater she had been working on, the one my sister had mentioned in her letter. And it was clear from the depression in the seat cushion, which gave the couch a tilted, half-capsized look, that my mother had been spending considerable time at her knitting post.

By sending me the letter, my sister, I believe, wanted to warn me about what I was going to find from my mother under the tree on Christmas morning. She knew me well enough to know that given my level of adolescent disaffection, I might not appreciate it in the way I should, and she was right. She was prescient, too, in thinking the superior attitude toward everyone and everything I had developed in advance of leaving for Connecticut College would have only increased from my exposure to East Coast ways. Faking surprise when I unwrapped the sweater wasn't difficult but I was taken aback to find the present unfinished, bright knitting needles hanging from it as if it was being acupunctured. But this discovery was soon absorbed by the fact that what I was holding was something I saw right away I would never wear—a big maroon rug of a sweater. "Oh, it's beautiful!" I must have exclaimed, and, "Just what I need." Fortunately, its unfinished state made it impossible to try on right then, although my mother asked me to stand up so she could hold it against my back and shoulders to check the fit. This saved her the embarrassment of discovering in front of everyone that she had made the collar too tight. Eventually, when it was finished, a few days before I returned to school, I would have to jigger the sweater down over my head from side to side with considerable force to get it past my nose and ears and then she would have to stretch and pull the shoulders into shape so that they fit the shape of my shoulders, which they were not designed to do. Most of the sweater's other dimensions were askew as well. The arms were as tight as blood pressure cuffs, the chest was nearly as snug, and the collar chafed and itched my neck and chin. It was also too long, extending below my crotch and covering part of my rear. (One of my girlfriends would use it later as a minidress.) But what was most wrong with the sweater was something I knew even before I had completely unwrapped it and no amount of stretching of shoulders, limbering up of the collar, or straightening of the hem could address. Instead of wool, my mother had used a synthetic yarn. It felt slippery and cheap, and it confirmed how thoroughly middle-class we were, as if it wasn't enough to be sitting in front of a Christmas tree, decorated with tinsel and small blinking lights, a trash bag for ripped-up wrapping and ribbons; the ribbons curled by the edge of a scissor blade. I didn't need to ask why she'd chosen acrylic or whatever it was. The answer was in my bones. It was less expensive than wool, although I wondered how much less, and even more to the point, more annoying, it was practical—machine washable. I hated it, the way I hated who I was, who I thought my parents were, and how and where I was raised, especially where, in a landscape devoid as the moon's, there were two moods: sunny and hot. In other words, my mother's hard work, her ambition—for this was the grandest sweater she would ever knit—her hope for keeping me warm, for protecting me against the cold she and my father long ago disavowed, and, quite frankly, her love for me was a reminder of my own disavowals, my dark, contrasting moods, and ambitions, and, finally, my difficulty acknowledging in more than chilly perfunctory ways that I, too, loved her.

Over the decades, on cold mornings, sometimes the sweater comes to mind and I'll rummage it out, imagining that if I try it on now, it will fit, as if the passage of time will have fixed its original flaws, but as I've gotten older my body has thickened, the sweater squeezes more and more like a Chinese handcuff and getting it over my head almost requires the help of my wife. But over time my antipathy and disaffection toward it has changed. What I've begun to feel about the sweater is no longer mixed up with the animosities I once harbored toward my mother. Instead, a kind of sadness for never having worn it the way it was intended has supplanted those feelings. It's not regret I feel because underneath the sadness is a sensation of gratitude, not so much for my mother's making of the sweater—the gesture of it—and not so much for the enduring fact of it, but I am grateful it has kept alive an unsolvable, uncomfortable, and ill-fitting problem. The one of how to accept the almost beautiful, imperfect life your mother gives you, woven out of her body, not from skill but by instinct, making not a second skin but the first and final one. The one that never feels quite like your own, the one whose material you would never choose for yourself, but which you spend your whole life putting on and taking off.

Hill Country Weavers
1701 South Congress Avenue
Austin, TX 78704
(512) 707-7396
www.hillcountryweavers.com

PAINTBRUSH LACE COWL

designed by Connie Devlin

Pattern designer Connie Devlin stays busy with her landscape and interiorscaping business but in her spare time she nurtures a passion for knitting lace. She loves working with color, texture, and patterns which she finds echoes her work laying out plant life.

THE SCOOP
Finished measurements
Version 1 (multicolor)
26" circumference and 18" tall, after blocking
Version 2 (solid gray)
24" circumference and 17" tall, after blocking

YARN

Version 1
Alchemy Silken Straw (100% silk; 236 yds/40g)
- 100 yds or 1 skein Tea Party (gold) (A)
- 100 yds or 1 skein Silver (gray) (B)
- 100 yds or 1 skein Montreat Path (brown) (C)
- 60 yds or 1 skein Rainforest (green) (D)
- 75 yds or 1 skein Equinox (orange) (E)

Alchemy Haiku (40% silk, 60% mohair; 325 yds/25g)
- 100 yds or 1 skein Tea Party (gold) (A)

- 100 yds or 1 skein San Francisco Sky (gray) (B)
- 100 yds or 1 skein Montreat Path (brown) (C)
- 60 yds or 1 skein Rainforest (green) (D)
- 75 yds or 1 skein Equinox (orange) (E)

Version 2
Alchemy Haiku (40% silk, 60% mohair; 325 yds/25g)
- 1 skein Silver

GAUGE

Version 1
abbreviations

cn	cable needle	**sl**	slip
k	knit	**st(s)**	stitch(es)
k2tog	knit 2 sts together	**yo**	yarn over
p	purl	**4/4 LC**	sl 4 sts to cn and
rep	repeat		hold to front, k4, k4
rnd(s)	round(s)		from cn

17½ sts and 27 rnds = 4" in Paintbrush pattern with 1 strand of each yarn held together, after blocking.

Version 2
21½ sts and 32 rnds = 4" in Paintbrush pattern with 1 strand of Haiku, after blocking.

NEEDLES

Version 1
One US #8 (5mm) circular needle, 16" or 24" long. Adjust needle size if necessary to obtain gauge.

Version 2

One US #3 (5mm) circular needle, 16" or 24" long. Adjust needle size if necessary to obtain gauge.

NOTIONS

Stitch markers in two colors, cable needle, tapestry needle, pins or wires for blocking.

STITCH PATTERNS

Seed Stitch (worked over a multiple of 2 sts) **Rnd 1:** *K1, p1; rep from * around. **Rnd 2:** *P1, k1; rep from * around. Rep Rnds 1–2 for pattern.

Paintbrush Pattern (worked over a multiple of 16 sts) **Rnds 1, 3, 5, 7, 9, and 11:** (Yo, k2tog) 4 times, k8; rep from * around. **Rnds 2, 4, 8, and 10:** Knit. **Rnd 6:** *K8, 4/4 LC; rep from * around. **Rnds 12, 14, 16, 18, 20, and 22:** *K8, (yo, k2tog) 4 times; rep from * around. **Rnds 13, 15, 19, and 21:** Knit. **Rnd 17:** *4/4 LC, k8; rep from * around. Rep Rnds 1–22 for pattern.

PATTERN NOTES

Throughout Version 1 of the Cowl, one strand of Haiku and one strand of Silken Straw in the same color are always held together and worked as one. For example; Color A in Silken Straw is always worked together with Color A of Haiku.

Version 2 is knit with a single strand of Haiku throughout.

Use one color of stitch marker to mark the beginning of the round and the other color to mark between each 16-stitch pattern repeat.

DIRECTIONS (VERSION 1)

With Color A yarns held together, cast on 112 sts using long-tail cast-on method. Place unique marker for beginning of rnd and join, being careful not to twist sts. Purl 1 rnd. Work 3 rnds in seed stitch.

Work Rnd 1 of Paintbrush pattern, placing markers between each 16-stitch repeat (7 times). Work through Rnds 1–22 of pattern 5 times in total, changing colors as follows:

First Repeat Rnds 1–8: Work with Color A. **Rnds 9–12:** Alternate Colors B and A each rnd. **Rnds 13–22:** Work with Color B.

Second Repeat Rnds 1–4: Alternate Colors C and B each rnd. **Rnds 5–20:** Work with Color C. **Rnds 21–22:** Alternate Colors D and C each rnd.

Third Repeat Rnds 1–2: Continue alternating Colors D and C each rnd. **Rnds 3–12:** Work with Color D. **Rnds 13–16:** Alternate Colors B and D each rnd. **Rnds 17–22:** Work with Color B.

Fourth Repeat Rnds 1–2: Work with Color B. **Rnds 3–6:** Alternate Colors E and B each rnd. **Rnds 7–18:** Work with Color E. **Rnds 19–22:** Alternate Colors C and E each rnd.

Fifth Repeat Rnds 1–8: Work with Color C. **Rnds 9–12:** Alternate Colors A and C each rnd. **Rnds 13–22:** Work with Color A.

Continuing with Color A, work 3 rnds of seed stitch. Purl 1 rnd. Bind off loosely.

FINISHING
Block to measurements with pins or wires. Weave in ends.

DIRECTIONS (VERSION 2)

With a single strand of Haiku, cast on 128 sts using long-tail cast-on method. Place unique marker for beginning of rnd and join, being careful not to twist sts. Purl 1 rnd. Work 3 rnds in seed stitch.

Work Rnd 1 of Paintbrush pattern, placing markers between each 16-stitch repeat (8 times). Work through Rnds 1–22 of pattern 6 times in total.

Work 3 rnds of seed stitch. Purl 1 rnd. Bind off loosely.

FINISHING

Block to measurements with pins or wires. Weave in ends.

PAINTBRUSH CHART

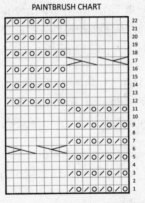

Note: Work all rows of chart from right to left.

KEY TO CHART

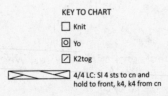

☐ Knit

◎ Yo

⟋ K2tog

4/4 LC: Sl 4 sts to cn and
hold to front, k4, k4 from cn

the unravelers

STEPHANIE MANNATT DANLER

As an unraveler, the author wants seams that do not tear.
But does she need to knit to get them?

T HERE ARE TWO KINDS OF WOMEN: THOSE WHO KNIT and those who unravel. I am a great unraveler. I can undo years of careful stitching in fifteen gluttonous minutes. It isn't even a decision really. Once I see the loose thread, I am undone. It's over before I have even asked myself the question: do I actually want to destroy this?

"My mother was a knitter," my Therapist says. She pauses. We've been seeing each other for so many years that we occasionally drift past the doctor-patient boundaries. I know that she is from New Hampshire and was an ice dancer. I know she's been married for thirty years or so, since her early twenties. Her husband can build a boat. I don't know anything about her mother.

Maybe it's the unseasonably mild November weather, or that her hair has grown back and she's not wearing a wig and she looks like herself again, but she continues.

"I have a story about knitting." She pauses again and glances at the clock to my right.

"That's wonderful because I have to write this thing about knitting. And knitting is like, a whole metaphor thing."

"A metaphor for what?"

"I think for life and fate. Also comfort. For love. For the divine feminine?"

She smiles and waits.

"So, I don't know yet. But it's one huge metaphor," I say finally.

My Best Friend is a knitter. My Best Friend can do everything. She's a mother, an entrepreneur, an excellent cook. She's considerate, spiritual, passionate. I know she's not perfect because I find perfect people irritating. She works harder than anyone I know. But from the view down here, she seems effortless.

She knits hats for her husband and son. She knit me a blanket one Christmas. It wasn't the first blanket she'd given me. I have known a lot of temporary beds and couches. The blankets are the comfort, the continuity, in what she calls my "gypsy" lifestyle.

My great-grandmother was a master unraveler. Her ring, the Snake Ring, is passed down to the eldest daughter in each generation, which it is my fate, my great privilege, to be. Let's examine the Snake Ring.

When David Taylor kissed Adelaide Barton after her USC graduation, she thought she was pregnant. So she married him. Adelaide had gone to college at sixteen and graduated in three years, but for all her precociousness, she was a true Victorian. The sun rose on Modernity quickly and made two girls, including my grandmother. But then Adelaide fell in love with her first cousin, Victor Barton. It helped that he was wealthy. She divorced David, a pharmacist who proceeded to dose and kill himself with his pills.

She married Victor and became Adelaide Barton Taylor Barton. Victor was sterile—"Thank God," my aunt says when she's recounting the story. He adopted Adelaide's two girls. By all accounts, he was a good man and father. They lived in a mansion in Hollywood and as a little girl my grandmother rode her horse onto the Paramount Studios back lot.

The wind shifted again and Adelaide told them she was moving to Vegas, alone. After thirty days she got another divorce. She left her daughters in Los Angeles in the care of friends and moved to Florida with a new lover, a ship captain named Edward Church, who incidentally had been her high school sweetheart. At forty-three she became pregnant and had another daughter. She and Edward put all their money into an oil freighter that ran aground on its inaugural voyage. She divorced him and gave the rest of her tiny bank account to her stockbroker. He was married. They had a twenty-year affair and she always made great returns.

For Adelaide's eighty-fifth birthday my aunt bought her red silk lingerie. The card said, "You need it." The retirement facility where Adelaide lived performed an in-house ceremony so she could get "married" to her boyfriend. He was one of three men still alive in the place. They couldn't make it official or they would both lose their social security. But Adelaide wanted to share his bed, and she did until he passed away in her arms a few years later.

Sometime between Edward Church with his doomed oil ship and her reign as resident tart of the old folks home, Adelaide took all of the diamonds from her wedding and engagement rings and turned them into a new ring. A snake.

"It's a phallic symbol," my aunt said to me. The ring had been hers. The eldest girl of her generation.

"It sounds cursed," I said. I was eighteen years old.

"Of course," she said. She dropped it into my hand. "The curse isn't the marriages. It's Adelaide's sex drive."

A LOOSE THREAD is a metaphor. Some examples of "loose threads":

Men with blue eyes. Men with green eyes. Bartenders with any-colored eyes. Bridge railings. Walks late at night. Perfectly cut lines of cocaine. Married men with blue or green eyes. A full bottle of pills, up or down. Credit cards. Airports, train platforms, bus stations, parking garages. The fourth glass of wine.

You don't feel that? The titillation of trouble? You must, even as a knitter. You wouldn't investigate. When you see a loose thread, you tie it off, or weave it back into the larger narrative so it's unnoticeable.

The loose thread shows us a flaw in what should be a perfectly plotted structure. They remind us of our own flaws—damage calling out to damage. A knitter is humbled by the reminder, but taps their needles together and forges ahead, straightly.

"It's not that you can't knit," said my Best Friend over the phone.

"So what is it?"

"It's that you don't even *try* to knit."

Ah. *Try*.

A REAL UNRAVELER develops a series of controls in order to live a productive life. Mine are in my spine. When I get scared I sit up straighter. I count my glasses of wine. I don't miss therapy. Unravelers are often certain that they have been fixed. They will tell you so with their eyes full of conviction. They are usually overinformed about their neuroses, and overperform in their profession. But at any second, it can go. Unraveling is all about the momentary pleasure, ignoring the losses unspooling to the ground. I can't lie; it is a dizzy, gorgeous freefall. The cleanup is awful.

WHEN MY THERAPIST'S mother was sick, she started a blanket. She was bedridden and it was a project for when she had the energy. Knowing that they were nearing the end of her mother's life, my Therapist said, Alright, it's time. I want to learn how to knit. She learned on that blanket as she watched her mother die. Towards the end, friends started to come by to talk and gossip, to say goodbye in that wizened, quiet way. The women that sat with my Therapist's mother picked up the blanket and added a few stitches. They passed it between them, the blanket expanding, evolving—

WHEN DOES A BLANKET become a blanket? Aristotle would need it to fulfill all its Causes. The first cause is material—the yarn in this case. The formal cause would be the spread of fabric, the blanket in the sick room. The efficient cause—or moving cause— would be the knitters, their hands specifically, which cause the material to take form. You would think that makes a blanket.

But it's not. Aristotle needs it to fulfill its Final Cause. Its purpose, so to speak. Warmth. When my Therapist tells me this story of a room of women knitting a blanket as death approaches, I understand that this blanket became a blanket even before it was finished.

MY FAMILY TALKS a lot about inheritance. They mean money, jewelry, real estate. My therapist talks about knitting as a kind of inheritance. The inheritance of the Snake Ring is something else entirely.

· · ·

EVERY FEW YEARS it seems, I call my Best Friend to have the same conversation. I sit in the middle of my apartment and survey my things.

"I have it again," I say to her. I am usually crying. "There's a boy."

My Best Friend drinks a green juice every morning. She doesn't drink wine or coffee anymore. Her eyes are illuminated. I can hear her son singing Taylor Swift in the background.

"You can just stop," she says, like a true knitter. "You don't have to throw your life away every time you get a crush. Just don't see him. Don't talk to him. Just stop."

"No, that's the point. I can't stop."

"Even my three-year-old can stop."

The needles click, click, the threads unravel, they trail on the floor between us while we grasp for a common language.

ONE MIGHT CALL unraveling "poor impulse control." That doesn't sound as sexy though.

I'M NOT AN expert, but I do have a fair imagination. Women who knit are able to sit still. They can sit with themselves for hours and not want to crawl out of their own skin. They can forget themselves for a minute and pick themselves back up again. They can give and not take.

My Best Friend tells me about being married: "It's not easy. But you have to stay focused on the larger picture. We are building something. You can't always get caught up in the minutiae."

Click, click go her knitting needles. She's pregnant again, with a girl this time, and she's knitting her a blanket.

"But all I see is the minutiae. The minutes," I say. Watching knitting is magic, the speed with which her fingers move, the way the stitches metastasize. "What if there is no larger picture? What if it's just these minutes? Minutes piled on top of minutes? I *feel* the minutes."

"It's not a quantity of minutes. The larger picture is a quality— it's a shape that holds. If you invest yourself in these feelings you'll lose your footing from one second to the next. You have to believe in what you're building, even if you can't make it out yet."

"Ah," I say. I sit back, defeated. "Now we're talking about faith."

THE FATES WERE flawed knitters. Well, that's not true. Two of them were great knitters: the one that spun the thread, and the one that measured it. But we all know what the third one was put there to do. Snip, snip.

MYOPIA DOESN'T SOUND awful. Hi, I'm myopic. It sounds dull, but at least not sociopathic. It sounds like something moths have when they fling themselves into windows, walls, bodies. They have no sense of their surroundings, no sense of strategy. They have other highly developed senses, don't they? Like a maniacal desire for light? Like an ability to find the source of that light and bear its unbearable heat? They certainly know how to make an exit, dusting the windows, walls, bodies with their wing prints and disappearing when the sun comes up, battering themselves— invisibly—into the sky to reach it.

LOOK, I'M NOT a total idiot. When I got married, I meant it. And I didn't marry one of these artistic, blue-eyed fuckups that tugged my loose thread.

I once married a green-eyed man. He knew all about me when he picked me up at twenty-three, coked out of my mind, wearing a key on my wrist so I could take the bumps easier. He knew about my boyfriend. He knew exactly what he was getting.

We thought we were different. He was a man who wore a suit and could see the forest through the trees. My tantrums, my despairs, my ennui, nothing could knock him off his course. He was tall. He never lied.

One winter day while I was cleaning I pulled my old Hawthorne off the shelf and read "Wakefield" again. "The man, under pretence of going on a journey, took lodgings in the next street to his own house, and there, unheard of by his wife or friends, and without the shadow of a reason for such self-banishment, dwelt up-wards of twenty years."

I put on my coat and my knitted hat and scarf, and I went to a bar I had never been to, and I ordered a gin martini, which I never drink.

We have lives layered on top of lives. The membrane between them is tissue thin. It was that martini that was the loose thread there. I sipped and could feel myself dropping out of my marriage, my integrity, my home, my career, my potential, and I sank into the barstool willingly.

Yes, my husband was different. I wasn't.

"How goes the knitting essay?" my Therapist asks.

"Not well," I say. I've picked my cuticles and she hands me a Kleenex because my thumb is bleeding. The hangnail, pick, pull.

"Have you figured out what kind of metaphor it is yet?"

I nod. I pull back more dried skin from around my thumb.

"It's a metaphor for everything I've ever failed at."

ADELAIDE, YOUR STORY is a little too cute for me. All that falling in love and jumping ship, all that leavetaking, sealing, lifting, cutting open the boxes, keeping one eye on the exit in every room. I'd like to ask you a few questions.

1. Did you get tired?
2. Did you ever knit your daughters a blanket?

When my marriage disintegrated I wanted to get addicted to Vicodin and sleep with any man that told me I had nice eyes. That would have been a real treat. Instead, I locked myself in a room, in a pitiful Bushwick sublet with five other roommates, got two jobs, and wrote a novel.

The secret is that writing the book was unraveling too. The minutes that turned into months and years were black. I had no faith. But the book will be published. And now people talk to me like I'm a knitter.

"You can fix almost anything in knitting. That's what keeps me going. It's not even hard," she says. "It's just about persistence."

"Do you hear yourself?" I ask.

"I know." She laughs. "Motivational speaking."

WHEN MY THERAPIST's mother passed they held a service. As my Therapist looked around the room, it took a moment for her to notice that many people had with them a pair of mittens or a scarf or a hat that was created by her mother's hands. For days after the service, people came up to her on the street to talk about how beloved those pairs of mittens, scarves, and hats were—some of these people were strangers. The objects had a second life and probably will have a third.

"NOW THAT," I SAY, "is a story about knitting."

I've started to wonder if there is anything in the world you can't turn into a metaphor. "I'm not a bad person, I'm a prettier metaphor for a bad person." I think about my Therapist's mother, and I wish that knitting was just knitting.

WHEN MY BOOK sold my Best Friend sent me a text: "EUDAIMONIA."

Aristotle says this is the Final Cause for us, our highest human good. The literal translation is something like having a good indwelling spirit. I always thought of it as a full-flowering of the soul. I thought it was joyful. I don't trust it anymore. This must be the hardest part of having unraveled a few times: joy can mean you've saved your life or you've ruined it.

Eudaimonia. I thought it meant to be aligned with your larger picture. I wear the Snake Ring where my wedding band used to be. So maybe, for better or worse, I am.

MY BEST FRIEND and I are in yoga. I'm lying on my back and the teacher tells me to shut my eyes. She tells me not to judge my thoughts. She asks me to imagine my best self.

I imagine myself knitting, and it feels like when I imagine myself praying: Lonely. I am in a white room, holding needles, and I tell myself to knit a whole new life that will hold its shape even if I turn my back. I want to knit woolly sweaters that will hold bodies—a husband, children, friends—and I want to knit seams that will not tear. But even in my own visualization, the needles are clicking, emptily.

Breathe, the teacher says. Really look at yourself. What do you look like?

I AM GOLD. I'm on a beach and I'm made of gold. There is a sun where my heart should be. Adelaide, do you know what you looked like? My chest is glowing. And all the people I've loved and lost are there. All the people I love and bear with me are there. I don't need to be touched anymore. My sun/heart pulses. From it comes a love that terrifies me. It rushes away from me like a tide. It comes back in a bronze, glittering wave, and covers us. Fuck the fucking knitting, I say in my head, and breathe.

handmade at home

JARED FLOOD

A lifetime of handmade clothing and a special gift from his father lead the author to a new realization about the importance of knitting and sewing.

I FEEL FORTUNATE TO HAVE GROWN UP IN A HOUSEHOLD where handmade clothing was a regular ingredient in everyday life. When I think back to my childhood, those pieces of my wardrobe that were lovingly made by my mother are the ones I remember most vividly. From warm Icelandic yoked pullovers knit in myriad shades of heathered wool to items that were more representative of the present decade (like neon "Hammer" pants complete with Velcro waistband pleats), from cotton shorts to button-up shirts tailored in matching fabric, my brothers and I were often swathed in one of Mom's creations. Though the clothes may not have seemed particularly special to us then, today I reflect on them with a much more appreciative air.

My mother is a veritable Swiss Army knife when it comes to crafting. She has always been driven by a desire to make things with her own hands, a trait that has lead to her mastery of a wide range of crafting disciplines. Sewing and knitting were always favored hobbies and I remember how she transformed our small walk-in pantry into a fully functional sewing room that she shared with our old washer and dryer. It was a humble place to work, and my mother's own private sanctuary in an otherwise rowdy house of boys. Her creations—hand-knit wool ganseys, button-down shirts in poplin broadcloth, warm blankets for cuddling with at nap time, even our own homemade versions of then-popular Cabbage Patch dolls and Care Bears—pepper my warm memories of childhood.

My father worked outdoors for the phone company as a telephone line repair and maintenance man and was often called out in the middle of the night for emergency repairs of town infrastructure damaged during heavy rain, wind or snow. The woolliest and most warming sweaters my mother saved for him, as his line of work (especially during rainy Pacific Northwest winters) was particularly well suited for the sturdiest of wool garments. Dad's fashion sense was very utilitarian; clothes needed to be hard-wearing and practical. For this reason, he too shared a unique appreciation for wool.

And speaking of wool—it was and still is my mother's true love. I certainly believe my own passion for this miracle fiber is in some part hereditary. My mother recounts how much more of an inconvenience her taste for wool was during the seventies and eighties, when yarns made of 100% natural fibers were hard to come by anywhere but a rare specialty yarn store. (Usually this statement is followed by another, in which she expresses her joy over the incredible abundance of natural fibers that are readily available to our knitting community today.)

In fact, there did come a time when my mother put knitting aside for a number of years simply because she lacked access to non-synthetic yarns. The only yarn shop selling 100% wool yarns in our small suburban town closed its doors, and with them my mom closed her knitting basket.

It wasn't until I found knitting while doing my undergraduate degree as an art student that my mother's latent passion for the craft awoke with new fervor, a passion that we quickly began sharing together. At the time I was attending college near my mother's home and we spent evenings (re)discovering the craft alongside one another. As time progressed and my involvement with knitting grew more serious, I became interested in hearing more about the wonderful hand-knits my mother had made for our family when I was younger. What patterns did she use, and what yarns? Which designers or brands was she loyal to in the pre-Internet era? Knowing her independent streak, I wondered how often she strictly followed a pattern versus deviating from instructions to make something completely her own (a preference we both share).

I was particularly curious about one of her hand-knits that I remember most distinctly (and one of many sweaters my mother made that I think contributed to the development of my own personal style). It was an epic, oversized shawl-collared cardigan she knit for my father in 1972. Worked in a bulky four-ply Cowichan wool, this sweater was serious business. With its deep raglan yoke and thick wooden buttons, the cardigan knit in a soft shade of heathered brown had authority of its own. The generously sized patch pockets fell perfectly at the wrists and acted as catchalls for tools or other miscellany needed for chores around the house or in the yard. The garment's most notable feature, however, was the magnificent ribbed shawl collar that added a subtle flair of drama and made the sweater irresistibly cozy.

I remember my father wore it constantly. He loved the thing. To me, it always seemed like the best kind of sweater—one that gives you permission to bring the comforts of home along with you when you venture out into the world—like wrapping up in your favorite blanket or bathrobe. A soft wool shield to keep you warm and comfortable wherever you might roam. A wearable nest.

What had happened to this garment? Did it still exist somewhere in the recesses of a dark attic or had it been passed along, as so often happened, to another member of our extended family at some indeterminate past moment? A few years earlier, my parents had decided to part ways, and while my mother was sure my father had probably not gotten rid of the garment, she couldn't say for sure where it might be hiding.

After finishing my undergraduate degree, I moved to New York City, entered the workforce, and after some time returned to school for my MFA. During my first year living in the city I started a blog to share and chronicle my own adventures with knitting, and hoped I might connect with a broader community of people who shared my love for the craft. Throughout my first few years of blogging I began designing and publishing my work both independently online and with some of the prominent pattern magazines in the industry. As I slowly became immersed in this new community and learned more about the knitting industry in our country, I started thinking about meaningful ways I might be able to contribute. These inner questions were the first steps in what was to become a larger textile journey of my own. By the following year, I had embarked on a personal project to create a small-batch U.S.-grown and -spun wool yarn for hand-knitters. I began this work in earnest while concurrently completing the final year of my master's program. It was an immensely full year as I spent virtually all of my free time doing research, planning and development for a project that I cared a lot about, and for which I had much to learn. Though I had been living in New York for just under five years by that point, I remember thinking that it was the first time I felt so far away from my family and the support system I had at home on the West Coast.

One rainy winter evening that year I was returning home from a week in New Hampshire; I'd spent the preceding days at a small, family-operated spinning mill there with whom I had been collaborating for the past few months. As sheets of icy rain battered the windshield, I parked the car halfway down the block and scurried quickly towards home and up the slick steps of the stoop to the front door of my building, where I caught a glimpse of something nestled snugly behind a potted plant. It was a simple parcel tucked away from the downpour all around. I reached to loosen the package from its hiding place and found it was addressed to me in my father's unmistakable, orderly penmanship. The parcel had a nice weight to it, though the contents seemed soft somehow—I had no idea what was inside.

Once in my apartment, I carefully opened the box to find my father's old, pillowy shawl-collared cardigan—the one I had been so curious about with my mother years earlier—safely stowed between two sheets of brown tissue and topped neatly with an envelope bearing my name.

Before opening the envelope, I removed the sweater from the box and threw it on over my clothes. It still looked as good as I remembered, and felt even better, especially on this dark winter evening. The smell of the sweater struck me suddenly, serving as a sort of time machine. I remembered rainy evenings with my dad returning late from another frigid job outdoors. He'd change into a dry set of clothes, crawl into this cardigan and begin a fresh fire in the woodstove. What a wonderful feeling being wrapped up (literally) in a memory!

I gingerly opened the envelope to reveal the hand-written sheets inside.

A two-page letter recounted my father's own memories of the sweater. Knit for him by my mother when they were young newly-weds, the garment had carried him through several winters as my parents began their family and raised three boys. He told me how warm and happy those years were—and how those memories, for him, had been knit directly into the fabric, much like the wool used to create it.

He reminded me that I was now the same age that he was during those fondly remembered periods; as I embarked on my own adult life he hoped this gift would bring similar experiences of joy, comfort and family into my own life.

With my mother's custom-embroidered "Handmade By" tag still clinging to the inside back neck of the garment, I consider it still to be one of the most special gifts I've ever received. Mostly because it is an object that so beautifully captures the generosity of spirit that both of my parents possess—my mother's thoughtful creation of the sweater, and my father's desire to pass down such a treasured object to me.

THERE ARE SEVERAL reasons to argue for homemade clothing. Making garments for yourself and your loved ones has always been a way to save money and weather difficult economic times while also providing the maker with the sense of provision and protec-tion over their family. Today it also provides a wonderful creative outlet for people interested in exploring a powerful avenue of self-expression, or mastering the skills of a timeless craft.

Important arguments can be made at the global level as well. Making our own clothes liberates us from supporting the disposable nature of the fashion industry. Our culture's obsession with "fast fashion" is wreaking havoc on our environment and sustains unethical and inhumane labor practices in countless countries around the world.

These are all great reasons to consider learning how to knit a sweater or sew a shirt, but the day I received that special cardigan from my father got me thinking of another meaningful reason I hadn't considered before.

We handmake our clothing also for the stories they'll tell. For the quiet legacies they inevitably create when passed on, linking one generation to next. With this act of creation we imbue a garment with layers of meaning from the moment of its very origin. Throughout its lifetime, additional layers accumulate as the garment tells its own story, just as my father's cardigan keeps me warm as I tell you mine.

wool

NICK FLYNN

*His grandfather was a wool merchant. Here, the author looks
at what his mother made from the scraps she received.*

*A loss of belief is what separates us from the much-handled
things we grew up with.*
—D. J. Waldie, *Holy Land*

A PAPER BAG, TEN SKEINS OF WOOL INSIDE. TWO BLOOD
red needles poke out from the open top. This is one of
the much-handled things I grew up with. A paper bag,
filled with enough wool—charcoal gray—for a sweater, if my
mother ever gets around to it.

My mother's name is Jody, her maiden name was Draper. Draper
is a name like Smith, it is the name of the thing the people do.
Smiths shoe horses. Drapers sell cloth. Her father, my grandfather,
was a wool merchant, as was his father, and so on, all the way back.

When my grandfather was a teenager he lived, for a summer,
on a sheep farm in Montana. After the war (World War II) he
would go back to that sheep farm, now as a journeyman merchant,
to learn the family business: how to grade the wool, how much to
offer for it, who to sell it to in the factories back east.

His youngest, his daughter (my mother), had been born just before the war. My grandfather held her, he must have held her, at least once, for at least a moment, before he shipped out. After the war, as he made his way back and forth to Montana, she grew up—she was what they called in the 1950s "rebellious." My grandfather and his wife were both drinkers, which limited their parenting skills and options, so at some point it made sense to simply ship Jody off to boarding school.

After the war this is what he didn't say: *Knee deep in the sea, waist-deep, my gun raised above my head, I was the one, slowly marching toward the fire, as the water slowed me, slowed us all. Back home my wife watched over our three children, the youngest, a girl, I hardly knew her, I was never able to know her, something always hung between us.*

A TROUBLED GIRL, a rebel, my mother was kicked out of one school after another, until she met my father, got pregnant, and took his name.

Penelope, weaving her tapestry in the day, unweaving it at night, attempting to slow time, to delay the moment she will have to decide.

I came home and I could never hold her, her hand so tiny in mine, her mouth so empty, as if all her teeth had been knocked out by the stock of a gun.

WHEN I WAS a boy I would take the P&B bus to Boston to visit my grandfather in his office. It would take about an hour; it cost about two dollars. I imagine my mother bought me the ticket but that might not be true—I did a lot on my own. The bus was silver and blue, the P stood for Plymouth (where the pilgrims landed), the B for Brockton, just another broken town to glimpse from the window of a moving bus.

The address of my grandfather's office was 10 High Street. The Draper Top Company. Top is a grade of wool suitable to knit. It has been combed, cleaned, spun into yarn. Sample skeins were lined up on a desk in his conference room, each skein had been touched by his hands, brought here from a ranch somewhere out west—by the end the wool was being imported from as far away as Australia. Some of the wool was sheep white, some dyed gray, some the black of a black sheep. Each was coiled like a tiny spool of rope, each wrapped in brown paper, a white label affixed to the paper. On the label: the date, the grade of wool, the farm of origin, all typed out neatly by his secretary.

Wool poked out from each end of the neatly wrapped skeins.

Skeins. The oil is what keeps the sheep dry, huddled in their field, rain and darkness falling. The oil is lanolin, it oozes from inside them, we use it to keep our hands soft, it waterproofs our boots. Every strand of wool has a tiny hook on each end, which hooks onto another strand when you roll them together. My grandfather explained this to me, using a finger from each hand to make two hooks—*Like this,* he said.

Men have a switch inside them—on, off, off, on—but the tracers, the fire, the blur, sometimes the button gets stuck . . .

Everyone speaks of the fire, but no one speaks of the wool—wool pants, wool jacket, wool socks—wool kept us warm, even waist-deep it held in our heat. But (sheep to the slaughter) it did not, could not, keep the fire from us.

I ASK MY DAUGHTER what she was before she was born and she says, *Nothing, I wasn't anything before this.*

WOOL MERCHANT—even as a child I thought he was out of time, as if he sold buggy whips, or wore a top hat. His father had made a fortune during the wars, back when all the uniforms were made of wool, all the blankets, all the felt lining in all the boots. If you had anything to do with wool you could become rich, and my great-grandfather did. By the time the Vietnam War was winding down polyester had slowly crept in, and slowly taken over. Wool would get eaten by moths, wool ended up with holes eaten into it.

My stepfather came home from Vietnam with a nylon camouflage blanket, which I would use for the rest of the 1970s—it rolled up small.

When I'd visit my grandfather, in his office, or anywhere, the first thing he'd do was to touch whatever shirt I was wearing, whatever sweater. He'd take a sleeve between his thumb and forefinger and rub it—in this way he would know if the sweater was pure, or a blend.

It was the 1970s, I wore polyester, I wore blends, we all did, but not around him.

I wish now I'd kept at least one label, if not an entire skein, but there were always so many—it seemed there'd always be a few lying around.

IN WAR NO ONE speaks of the ones who are already down, already on their knees, the ones not yet to the beach and already fallen into and maybe under the water, under the waves, which will not save them. No one speaks of the man using his gun as a crutch, the man using his gun as a shield, the man who has already abandoned his weapon. None of these men will make it, empty-handed almost, their eyes, we will never see their eyes, not as they move into the fire, into the smoke. Explosions and fire and smoke, flashes of light which signal a death, then another. The water is up to our waists, which is good, as we are pissing ourselves empty. I hold the gun above my head, we all have the same rifle. We all have the same helmet, we all have the same boots, we are a unit and we move as a unit through the waist-deep sea. Waist-deep a hundred yards from shore, we hold our rifles above the water, we move as one, in our wool suits, the shore simply a noise we cannot hear, a hundred yards into the distant blur.

Think of it: not only were we moving toward the light, we were becoming light.

WE ALWAYS KNEW that if we wanted to knit anything we could have gotten all the wool we'd need from him. If we had wanted to we could have knit eternally, there was no end to the amount of wool we could have had.

What we got was one paper bag filled with charcoal gray skeins—I had picked out the color, it was to be a sweater for me, my mother was going to knit it.

Then, for years, we moved this paper bag around the house, trying to find a place for it, somewhere that would insist. It was on the list of projects but it was a project forever delayed. *No sense in knitting something you will outgrow in a year.*

BEFORE THERE WERE fields there was ocean, it covered the fields and what died inside became earth. Before there were oceans there were stars, one exploded and the oceans rained down. Before sheep there were wild sheep, they lived in the forests, the men came and captured them, their fleece so matted, it grew so long it dragged on the earth, thick with brambles. Men invented knives to shear them, invented the comb to brush it out, let the sheep run naked through the fields, which had been coral gardens a million years before . . .

· · ·

MY MOTHER'S SIDE of the family came over from England to Massachusetts in the mid-1800s, opened a wool mill in Canton. If you go to Canton today the name Draper is still on many buildings, there is still a Draper mill. If you go inside you will find machines, looms, invented by my relatives, the name Draper stamped onto each one. But by the time I knew my grandfather the bottom had fallen out. When I'd go to his office he'd be at his desk, looking into a blank screen. He'd be on the phone, talking to another old guy, a crony from the old days. *Five hundred skeins of Wyoming grade A mohair top*, and the crony would take it off his hands. On the walls of his office were etchings of sheep, Currier & Ives, men with top hats lining the pens. This was the world, and then it changed. In this way all the money passed down from all those wars passed through his hands and flowed out the hole in the bottom.

SOMETHING BETWEEN US . . . maybe that war.

Yet this is the truth about the war: my grandfather came from money, and so he would never see combat—he was a Seabee, construction brigade—his job was to supply the ships with food, with clothes. His war was far from the bombs, from the fires, from the blur.

And so he came home from his war, her hand so tiny in his. Remember: before she defied him, before she brought shame, before she went off with one of the men who dug ditches in town, she was a child. Then, just as my grandfather was leaving his wife for his secretary at the Top Company (*Meet me in Reno, love, and we will begin our new life*), Jody got pregnant—she was seventeen. Years later, when I am twelve, she will take another man (the Vietnam vet)'s name, which left us, her and I, with different names. Then, four years later, when he left, she went back to her father's name, her maiden name, but even this was not back far enough. So one day she took one more step back, to a time before she was born. As if Penelope, by her unweaving, finally reduced—returned— the tapestry back into a few skeins of wool.

If it had been possible to put the wool back onto the sheep I believe my mother would have done it.

THE WOOL HAD waited, for years, in its paper bag, the two red needles poking out of the top. My grandfather would ask about it, at our monthly lunches in his mansion, the mansion he inherited from his father. My mother needed to make something with what she'd been given, before she'd be given anything more.

Currier & Ives on the walls. A bookcase lined with porcelain sheep. A wine cellar. Six crackers on a plate, enough for two apiece. Madame Defarge, keeping track of the beheadings with each knot.

I'd wear one of the plaid Pendleton shirts my grandfather gave me for Christmas each year. That way he wouldn't even have to touch it to know it was pure, but still, he touched it.

At one point my mother picked up the blood red needles and began, she must have taught herself. I can remember the sweater, I wore it constantly—charcoal gray, cable knit on the front— but I cannot see her sitting still long enough to make it. I cannot remember when it was new but I remember the end of it, the elbows, blown out from wear. By the end it was simply, again, little more than a pile of yarn. One sweater, out of all those sheep, all that wool, all those factories, all those looms.

Even after the elbows were blown out I put it in mothballs and pulled it out only for the monthly lunches, which near the end were more like every other month, at that. That chemical smell hung off me as I sat in the mansion—could everyone smell it or just me?

By now I was drinking and he once even offered me a beer, but I didn't stop at one. Cables down the front, the sleeves too long, from wool he'd graded himself from a ranch I never saw in Montana—this was the uniform I wore to his house, until the end.

Look at what I have made, my mother might have uttered, *from the scraps you have offered.*

why, yes—i *can* knit my way out of a wet paper bag . . .

DIANA GABALDON

If the author of the Outlander *novels hadn't quit the 4-H Club as a young girl, would the popular Starz television show still have created such a knitting craze?*

I LEARNED TO KNIT IN ORDER TO SPITE THE 4-H.
When I was in—I think—the sixth grade, a classmate named Linda Zanzucchi invited me to join a 4-H group her mother was about to lead. Linda had eleven brothers, and her mother tried as hard as possible to carve out a little feminine time for Linda amid the surging maelstrom of testosterone chez Zanzucchi, hence the 4-H cooking class.

We had fun in the first year of the class, starting with Purple Cows and progressing to chocolate chip cookies. Purple Cows were a natural for Mrs. Zanzucchi; the Zanzucchis owned the local dairy and they had—wonder of wonders—a huge cafeteria-style milk dispenser in their kitchen (*vide* the twelve kids). (Should you ever want to make a Purple Cow, it consists of equal parts milk and grape juice, with a half-part of 7UP and a dollop of vanilla ice cream. Very nutritious and it tastes a whole lot better than it sounds.)

In the second year, though, Mrs. Zanzucchi passed the reins to a lady whose name I don't recall, who went by the book—the 4-H recipe book, that is. We found ourselves compelled to make—and eat—tamale pie (I'm Hispanic; to me, tamales are tamales and pies are pies and never the twain shall meet. Besides, cornbread made from a mix and canned sloppy joe didn't strike me as edible, no matter *what* you called it), stuffed bell peppers (stuffed with bread crumbs and canned sloppy joe goop; the 4-H recipes were big on ground beef in all its permutations, but particularly when covered with toxic red tomato glop), and a lot of other things I didn't think were food. I also didn't see much point in slavishly following recipes. (My dad was, among other things, a professional chef. I often watched him at work, and the mysteries of the kitchen didn't seem to me like something requiring a handbook.) So I quit.

Come the next year, and the 4-H put out their list of classes, among which was a knitting class. I thought that sounded interesting, so I signed up. Whereupon someone from 4-H called my mother and explained—more or less tactfully—that since I'd quit the last class, they weren't disposed to risk my doing it again, and therefore wouldn't let me join the knitting class (or anything else ever again, was the implication).

The 4-H doesn't like quitters, and I don't hold that against them. On the other hand . . . neither do I. I may choose—for good and sufficient reason—not to continue doing something, but that doesn't make me a quitter.

So, I reasoned, if they thought you could learn to cook from a book, then plainly you could learn to knit from one, too. So I asked for a knitting book, yarn and needles for Christmas, and got them. Spent the Christmas holidays teaching myself to cast on, knit and purl, and made a stylish (not) pair of slippers, in green/brown/yellow-shaded four-ply acrylic (it came with the book) with number 8 needles. I wore these, *pro forma*, for a few days, but as I'd also received for Christmas a jazzy pair of pink bedroom slippers with pink fur around the ankles, I quietly stuffed my first knitting project into the bag of clothes bound for St. Vincent de Paul. (I can't imagine what the deserving poor thought about them, but at least they were off my conscience.)

I had the bug, though, and began saving my allowance and birthday money to buy yarn. I got a book of 100 Popular Knitting Stitches, which fascinated me, and made sampler squares of all of them (this being interesting but requiring a very modest amount of yarn). It also taught me that while fancy stitches are entertaining and ornamental, the virtue of a knitted garment lies mostly in its structure, color and texture. (If you choose to think this perception contributed to the way I write books, you're entirely welcome to do so. Everything you experience forms you as a writer. Why should knitting be an exception?)

When I acquired a serious boyfriend in college, I invested the not-inconsiderable effort of knitting him a fisherman sweater, cable-stitched in cream wool (it *was* a considerable effort, too, as he was sizable). We got engaged, and then I fell instantly and madly in love with a tall, redheaded French horn player whom I sat next to in the Northern Arizona University marching band. I broke the engagement, and made stylish patterned sweater vests for the horn player. I also married him, and nearly killed him by knitting him a sweater made of natural hand-spun New Zealand wool, which he wore to please me. It was cold in Flagstaff, Arizona, but not *that* cold, and he nearly died of heatstroke. (He could have crossed Antarctica in that thing in perfect comfort—provided I had also knitted him a pair of pants in the same yarn.)

After that, life got busier and we lived in Los Angeles, where one might possibly require warm socks for a week or so, once a year. My knitting became sporadic, until we moved to Phoenix and I began to volunteer for a charitable organization called Recording for the Blind and Dyslexic.

RFB&D is exactly what the name indicates; their mission is to make audio recordings of materials that print-handicapped people need for educational or business purposes. (They used to be called "Recording for the Blind," but in fact, only about ten percent of the clientele is non-sighted. "Print-handicapped" means anyone incapable of reading a book, for any reason—including muscular dystrophy or cerebral palsy, which might make holding a book for long periods impossible, as well as learning conditions such as dyslexia.)

I was a volunteer reader for Recording for the Blind & Dyslexic for some twenty-seven years, and while my value to that organization lay in my ability to read passages like ". . . producing alga with many free-living species, especially common in crustose tropical lichens: *Coccomyxa,* a common terrestrial alga, occurring in the common green species of *Peltigera* and *Solorina* and the mushroom lichens, *Dictyochloropsis,* common in *Lobaria* and *Pseudocyphellaria* . . ." at a speed of 240 words per minute (the normal person reads aloud, I'm told, at 120 wpm),[1] that ability depended on my staying awake through the less exciting passages.

[1] When I started volunteering at RFB&D, they told me that most people can listen much faster than most people can talk. This is why people tend to drift off during long lectures; the information coming in through their ears isn't occupying enough of the space between them, and the unoccupied parts of the brain go looking for something else to do. Clients of the foundation were equipped with special players which could speed up the recordings to as much as three or four times normal speed (your iPod or phone will speed up to twice normal), so they could adjust their listening speed for maximum efficiency. Doing this, though, raises the pitch of the recorded voice, so above a certain level, it becomes too squeaky to listen to comfortably. Hence the value of a naturally fast reader.

The difficulty, though, was that the only time I could read for them—fitting it in between work and family—was on Wednesday mornings, and I Am Not a Morning Person. Passages such as ". . . it is easy to see how *Hydrodictyon* can form such conspicuous blooms in nature. Sexual reproduction in *Hydrodictyon* is isogamous, and meiosis is zygotic, as in all sexually reproducing *Chlorophyceae*" were sufficiently challenging as to keep me awake at 9 a.m., whereas *Basic Principles of Economics* would make me nod off in seconds—and audible yawning is Frowned On while you're doing this sort of reading.

So I took to bringing my knitting with me to the studio. The mental and physical effort required to knit was enough to keep me awake, and while I naturally couldn't do things involving counted-stitch patterns, multiple needles or lots of increase/decrease while reading, I could knit afghans or the little Oxfam children's sweaters with no problem at all.

I became something of a celebrity—well, more of a side-show freak, to be honest—and the RFB folks would bring new volunteer prospects back to gawp at me through the window of my recording booth, and would call the local newspaper to come out and photograph me *in flagrante*, as an accompaniment to their annual fund-raising article.

But then I began to write novels, and life changed again. I quit my job at the university, I gradually stopped writing for the computer press, and my kids got older[2] . . . but at the same time, my books got

---

[2] The kids were six, four and two when I began to write novels. They're now thirty-two, thirty and twenty-eight. My eldest daughter reached high school and didn't join the 4-H, but did ask me to teach her to knit. I did, whereupon she flew past me and in no time was turning out beautiful matched skirts and capelets in bamboo colorways, asked for a spinning wheel one Christmas and a niddy-noddy the next, and when last seen was happily feeding the alpacas at a farm outside Portland (where she now works as an OR nurse. The job involves a lot of sitting around, so she's been able to keep the whole family in bamboo socks). Thanks

popular. And more popular. And MORE popular . . . Mind you, this is definitely a Good Thing, but an unforeseen side effect of such visibility is that people want you to be still more visible. They want to see you, listen to you, and touch you (I *think* it's an effect of the "show" textiles I wear when addressing the multitudes rather than the fact that I look small and deceivingly cuddly),[3] but people are inclined to pet me. And as I routinely say to injudicious audience members at book signings who express impatience as to when the next book is coming out: "Well, you've got a choice. You can have the next book sooner—or you can look at me. (*pause*) Are you lookin' at me?"

I learned to deal with the mountain of increasing requests for appearances, signed books, photos, interviews, etc., and then—

They made a TV show out of my books, and my relationship with knitting acquired a Whole New Dimension.

The premium cable channel Starz acquired the film rights to the whole series of *Outlander* novels, and filming began in October of 2013, in Cumbernauld, Scotland. And long before the first episode was released, the world was ravished, not only by the glorious landscapes and riveting actors, but by the costumes designed by Terry Dresbach. And particularly by the knitted accessories adorning those costumes!

From the moment Claire appeared in her dramatic knitted cowl in Episode 3, needles began to click in inspired imitation.

---

to her influence, I now own a much higher-quality to-be-knitted pile than heretofore, full of alpaca magenta colorways and something white that's meant to be knitted into a cuddly bunny rabbit, which will probably happen about the same time my first grandchild is born. I.e., not anytime soon . . .

[3] As my son—himself a published novelist (Sam Sykes, *The City Stained Red* is his most recent book)—once remarked to me, "People think you're this cuddly little Hobbit . . . but you're *not*."

Add in the lovely shaped capelets, Mrs. Fitz's hand warmers and the Highlanders' Scotch bonnets, and Etsy exploded.

Now, owing to the fragility of textiles and the harshness of life in the Scottish Highlands, there's very little clothing that has survived from the eighteenth century. Scraps of tartan—most of them purporting to be from Bonnie Prince Charlie's philabeg—are to be seen in some great houses, but there's not much in the way of common people's clothing, let alone knitted articles like stockings, that had a lot of wear.

Still, we know that people did *wear* stockings in the eighteenth century; we can see them in paintings of the period, and they're referred to in literature. Ergo . . . people knitted. Actually, almost everyone knitted; I can't at the moment recall where I saw it, but I did see a description of a man and wife walking along together, each knitting at one end of a shared large garment. Still, portraits are scarce, and there's no telling exactly what knitted garments might have been worn, besides stockings. Plainly there's a great deal of creativity in the *Outlander* costumes; they're based very strongly on actual garments of the period—nobody knows costume history like Terry does!—but aesthetic liberties can certainly be taken in the details, and the overall effect is gorgeous.

I haven't—yet—tried knitting any of the *Outlander* garments myself, but I was sent a pattern for Dougal's bonnet, which I have it in mind to do for my husband, as soon as I find a yarn more suitable than the magenta alpaca (yes, it would make it easier to spot him in snow, but he wouldn't wear it, and it doesn't usually snow that much in Scottsdale, Arizona).

I can't take any personal credit for this Scottish-themed explosion of interest in knitting (knitting had been increasing in popularity for years before *Outlander* came along), but I am kind of gratified, not only by the enthusiastic admiration for Terry's designs, but by the astonishing growth of sites like Outlander Pattern Central (on Facebook), where people contribute their own versions of the costume patterns (and anything else that comes to mind as a result).

I do sometimes wonder what might have happened if the 4-H had thrown me out of a class on poultry-raising or tractor maintenance, though.

the red vest

DEBRA GWARTNEY

*Remembering the gift of a knitted red vest leads the author to
examine her family's rule to keep its troubles to itself.*

O N THE FIRST DAY OF FIRST GRADE, A LONG TIME
ago now, my grandmother came into my room in our
house in Idaho to give me a present. It was a red vest,
size small for small me, that she'd knitted herself. I climbed out of
bed while she held it up to the light of the window, a woolly tube
I suspected would bind me like a foot in winter, itchy and damp. I
already dreaded wearing it.

But I wouldn't tell her so. Even if a gripe knocked against my
teeth, I would have licked it away. *Keep your troubles to yourself* was
the main tenet around our house, with parents who tolerated no
shade or volume of complaint—if you whined about a canker
sore in your mouth, our father packed your gums with alum; if
you stayed home with a bellyache, our mother looked you up and
down and said, "If you're not barfing you're well enough to empty
the dishwasher." And when Mamie visited with our grandfather,
we four children stayed in tiptoe mode: no unhappy word spoken
to possibly upend her.

In my room, I reached up to finger the ribbing along the bottom of the vest, reminding myself that, really, I wanted only to please this grandmother who often ran her fingers through my hair to soothe me out of worry and who once sent me red Mexican jumping beans from Tijuana that I let rot under my bed until the cat ate them. This grandmother who cooked up hot lemonade and sat at the edge of my mattress spooning it down my throat until whatever fever broke.

My mother hovered in the doorway while her mother helped me try on the vest. As I slipped my arm through a hole, I noticed Mamie's lip pulsing in one corner, a twitch I recognized from other times she was unsettled, and she was frequently so. Now I'd carry a worry about what was bothering Mamie into the day. I'd fuss and pick at what I might have done to cause her this upset and the chewing out my mother would lay on me later if I said the wrong words about Mamie's gift. Still, I remember I wasn't tempted to ask my grandmother the cause of her sadness. This in accordance with another of our family codes: if you must indulge in suffering, suffer in silence, and, please, let others do the same.

IT WAS STRANGE that Mamie had chosen to knit for me, her oldest grandchild. Aunt Sue, Mamie's younger sister, was the famed family knitter. These two women, whose competition was legion, tended to keep each to her own ground. My grandmother was best at boiling chokecherries into purple syrup to soak into stacks of sourdough pancakes; she was best at catching a fat steelhead from the Salmon River near her house and grilling it up for dinner, picking out bones kids might choke on. She was good at using her pointy scissors to cut my hair and my sisters' into summer pixies.

While Sue, who lived one state over, mostly stayed clear of the kitchen and she kept herself miles from forest or river. Her prowess was knitting sweaters with straight collars and perfectly matched sleeves. My great-aunt drew wool from a frumpy bag that sat next to her creaking rocking chair after she plopped down and flipped off her white shoes to rest her *dogs*, home from a grave-yard shift of nursing at the hospital. She mostly avoided commotion around her—her four children and visitors, my siblings and me—by focusing on slipstitches and cast-offs. Aunt Sue darted her fingers, looped and clicked, a mitten forming between her hands, a brown sock unfurling in her lap. As her needles clacked, she usually joked with whoever was around her, a humor my grandmother called *naughty*, that I'd later call *ribald*. But if her mood was dark, Sue's jabs were as sharp as her jokes—you're too loud, you dropped crumbs on my rug, you smell like a dog in an alley. And if Mamie was around, the criticisms were usually pointed directly at her.

My question back then, even when I was too young to have language to form such an inquiry, was this: Why did my grandmother just stand there and endure Sue's rants and scoldings?

Sue had survived her husband's death in his mid-thirties—a brain tumor that booted the door in one day and killed him before anyone could blink. She did so by barreling straight through grief. She'd always been the tell-it-like-it-is member of the family, feisty and daring, and as a widow she became a ball of fury. Aunt Sue had been cheated out of domestic contentment, and she seemed to expect everyone to pay with about an inch of hide.

And then there was my grandmother. Four of the five babies she gave birth to died. After the last one, Mamie folded in on herself. No, she collapsed in on herself. She didn't roar like her sister, she didn't let out the grief that seared her. Instead, she reminded me of a bicycle caught under a car's tire, spokes that would never be right again no matter how many times they were straightened. And who wouldn't be crippled? Twin boys born a month early, too small to make it. Two years later, a boy, followed a year or so later by a girl, both born bright-eyed and plump but dead within hours. Eventually my grandmother's Rh-negative blood was tapped as the cause—the fatal crossing of maternal and infant blood at the moment of birth. After the last child's burial, the girl who was laid by her brothers under a tombstone that read "Budded on Earth to Bloom in Heaven," Mamie stopped writing her name. She didn't deserve a name, she said. To the end of her life she was *Mrs. Ronald Burke*, as if the young woman named Mae had been prevented from blooming, too.

I DON'T REMEMBER being told not to bring up the babies. I just knew not to. Absolutely no word about the infants, not ever. In the forty-five years I was around her, Mamie spoke not a single time about her dead children, though Sue talked in offhanded ways about her husband, the man she at once glorified and condemned for ditching her. I never heard the sisters quarrel about these big losses—who'd had it worse—though they kept each other riled about everything else, a back-and-forth spar with the pettiest of stakes. One accused the other of making the coffee wrong again, too gritty or thick. They fought over the right way to hem a pair of pants or stew a chicken or space tulip bulbs in the garden. They argued throughout every one of their visits. Sue snarled and Mae whimpered. They flew apart and, minutes later, returned to go at it again, as if they couldn't stop. As if were they to quit their same old pattern, they'd simply dissolve.

I remember Aunt Sue at our house once. The night she arrived she pulled me out of bed, from under my covers. My feet were dirty, she insisted. How had she known? She dragged me to the bathroom, Mamie right behind, where she made me sit on the edge of the tub. From her blue Samsonite case, whose fasteners snapped with an authority that suited her, Aunt Sue brought out a wire brush mean as a weasel. I watched in horror and a modicum of fascination as rolls of skin sloughed off my feet, drowned under water gushing from the faucet. When the scrubbing went deep enough to hurt, turning my toes purple, I waited for my grandmother to step in. Wasn't Mamie going to keep Sue and her brush from peeling another layer from me? I must have been nine or ten at the time, old enough to bristle at my grandmother for not swooping me away from Sue. But not old enough to be aware of my own predilection, a habit of doing nothing to protect myself. Even then it was hard-wired. I didn't ask Aunt Sue to ease up, I didn't yank my foot away from her. I dried off and went to bed seething that no one had saved me.

ALL THIS IS TO SAY that, despite a staunch reluctance to invade Sue's territory, my grandmother had knitted. For me. That day in my room, when I was six years old, I fidgeted with the vest too snug around my nightgown. *Can I take it off now, please?* The glance at my mother was meant to convey this request, and from the doorway, she shot back her own stare to remind me to ladle thanks onto my grandmother and to let no hesitation creep in. So I wrapped my arms around Mamie's waist and I said words about the vest loud enough for my mother to hear. *I'll never take it off.*

An hour later, when I walked between my mother and grandmother to the bus stop, Mamie's vest did make for a comforting layer. But then I stepped onto a bus sardined with flighty children; I tumbled through hours of giddy teachers, crowded playgrounds, spelling tests and math exercises, an imposingly tall principal who roamed the halls. The day was warm and my skin turned to crab grass, to prickly pear. When the teacher sent us out to last recess, I hurried onto the asphalt hoping for a breeze, but the air was still and the sun bore down on the sweaty lot of us. I huddled next to a pole, under the shadow of a tetherball, and pleaded with myself to take off the vest. For only a few minutes, the mere span of this recess. I needed a respite from the wool that clung to me like a Brillo pad. My right hand even made its way to the buttons, but I couldn't move my fingers to undo them. My mother, my grandmother. They wanted me to keep it on, this vest, Mamie's prize, proof of my loyalty, my grandmother's reason to call Sue and report on the granddaughter who'd worn, all day on the first day of school, a piece Mamie had knitted herself.

Sue would not have been all that impressed. In her book, you did what you had to do and didn't wait around for praise. When her husband died, Sue lived on the East Coast. Mae and the rest of the family still lived in Idaho. Sue sold her house, packed her things, made her way to Washington State. She worked nights while her children slept. She slept herself while they were at school. She asked for nothing.

And every time Mamie went into labor, no matter where she lived at the time, Sue got herself to the hospital. She arrived before the babies were born, my mother who lived and the others who didn't. Sue was next to the bed, helping the doctor with her official RN degree and her soft white shoes. She was there to manage things for Mae, who *never did know how to stand up for herself.*

Once when I was visiting my aunt and grandmother, I watched Sue pound her way into the kitchen, a finger out to poke in Mamie's face, who, Sue insisted, had stirred too much butter into the mashed potatoes. Mamie said nothing, but shrank into her same dim corner, her forehead cracked like stomped-on ice. That night, I thought about my aunt's insistence at being at the babies' deliveries, her Navy nurse stoicism squaring her shoulders. I wondered if my grandmother would have preferred to be alone, with her husband in the hallway and the doctor at her side, without this sister's nattering voice in her ear about getting over another dead child.

If so, why couldn't she say so?

By the time I had such thoughts I was a new mother myself. Sue lived in a mobile home across town from me, her children long grown, retired now from her nursing job. Under her chair was the same bag of yarn and needles—acrylic yarn now, cheaper than wool and, she told me, more resilient. Her hands clickity-clacked in the pale living room of her sparsely furnished double wide, a lone photo of her husband atop a bookcase. She knitted as she watched TV so that the flickering light across her arms made it seem like clouds were passing over.

Some days, I left my baby, Amanda, with my visiting grandmother and Sue and took a few hours for errands. When I returned, Aunt Sue usually answered the door with a clenched jaw, her mouth a stubborn line across her face. She'd throw herself back in her chair and start knitting again, knitting as if mending a hole in the world, knitting as if she was fixing us—or at least repairing the quarrel she and Mamie were in the middle of that afternoon. I'd find Mamie stirring nothing into another cup of coffee at the far reaches of the kitchen, or in the back room patting my sleeping daughter's back. I'd gather up my child and the bag of diapers and toys and hurry away before aunt or grandmother could suggest I pick a side.

One August day, pregnant with a second daughter and with toddler Amanda playing on Aunt Sue's rug, I stayed in with the women who were by then in their mid-sixties. I stretched over one of Sue's soft chairs, a fan blowing in my face. Mamie sat nearby, chattering with my daughter. Despite the heat, Sue was knitting. Maybe because my bulge of a belly was obvious in the room—who knows—Aunt Sue began, out of nowhere, to talk about Mamie's babies. I couldn't at first compute what she was saying, so startling were her words, but then I did. *Those first boys, those twins of Mae's.* Sue went on as if this wasn't an unbreachable topic. As if the woman who was to never hear a word about her dead children wasn't sitting in the room. I wanted to leave, scoop up what belonged to me and rush away. That's all I could think of doing, to run.

Next to me, Mamie stared straight ahead, her hands wrung in her lap. Amanda began to whimper and I picked her up. I said *shh* into her hair, though it was Sue I wanted to hush. But my great-aunt continued, describing how, in the last moments of labor, a nurse had pressed a gauze pad soaked with ether against Mamie's mouth and nose. While Mamie slept, Sue saw the boys born, one after the other. While Mamie slept, the babies cried. Sue described wrapping the twins in blankets to carry to the nursery while Mamie shook herself from the anesthetized fog. Sue alone sat next to the Isolettes that held the children—separated from their mother, separated from each other—until they died.

I gave Amanda a toy and set her back on her blanket so I could turn toward my grandmother. To do what, I didn't know. I wanted Mamie to yell. I wanted her to get up and shake her sister. To break windows, throw her cup across the room. But Mamie did nothing, she said nothing. And I said nothing, too.

I now see that Sue's intentions that day were aligned with her way of being in the world—*Let's get this thing out in the open and finally talk about it.* At the time, I missed that by a mile. It was only Mamie's intentions I could recognize, because I was stuck there, too: Keep it in, don't talk about it, don't bother others with your troubles. Keep it in like a balloon filled with poison in your belly, waiting for the moment the balloon finally bursts.

MANY YEARS BEFORE that day at Sue's house, I got off the bus at the end of the first day of first grade and walked the couple of blocks home. My mother was in the kitchen, and when I found her there, she took my lunch pail and opened it. I heard my sisters and brother in the backyard, Mamie with them. I was about to run outside, too, when my mother told me to first change my clothes. It was in that moment that she and I both realized I was not wearing the vest.

"Where is it?" she said.

I didn't know, I told her, though it dawned on me that I'd left it on the bus. My mother grabbed my arm, hustled me into the hot back bedroom I shared with my sister, ensuring my grandmother couldn't hear our exchange. "Do you have any idea how long she worked on that?" she said. "She stayed up past midnight so you could wear it today. Do you know what this is going to do to her?"

Then she was gone, my mother, to begin a futile effort at recovery, calling the school, the bus company. I stood alone in the bedroom, the white blouse stuck to me like plastic wrap, my feet swollen in unforgiving shoes. How would I tell Mamie that I, too, had let her down? Then a solution occurred to me, the sweetness of relief unlocking my knees so I could lower myself to the bed. I didn't have to tell her. I didn't have to explain that the heat of the bus was unendurable, and that I'd finally given in and stripped off the vest. I'd say nothing. The beautiful nothing. Without an inkling I'd just signed on to my family's pact, I chose to stay silent. I'd pretend the vest never existed and I'd trust its loss would drift away like so much steam.

It's been half a century since I left the vest in the bus, gathering up my pail and satchel and hurrying off into the sunshine. I never spoke of it again to my grandmother, nor she to me. It's been about three decades since I didn't move from my chair at Sue's house, since I failed to walk across the living room to say *stop*, or to say *go on, tell us more*. To say anything at all.

I never asked my grandmother, even on her deathbed, about her lost children, and she never brought them up to me.

And that vest my grandmother knitted for me: I haven't forgotten it. How could I? It's a sliver under my skin that still festers. Sometimes I even think about the bus returning to the shelter that afternoon, the driver strolling through to gather detritus left by children, ham sandwiches, current events quizzes, wadded Kleenex. On a seat halfway back, she finds twisted in a knot a red vest with three smooth buttons. She holds it up, shakes it out. *Handmade*. Not an expert job, but good enough to give the neighbor girl. She folds it into a pocket to take home. She doesn't feel bad claiming it. After all, who would ever miss such a small thing?

Churchmouse Yarns & Teas
118 Madrone Lane North
Bainbridge Island, WA 98110
(206) 780-2686
www.churchmouseyarns.com

CHEERY SEED STITCH TEA COZY

A tea cozy will keep water hotter while steeping and the tea warm while you finish "just one more row." Choose a wool yarn for best insulation. Dark colors, tweeds, and multicolored yarns are great for hiding drips. Knit a wardrobe of jaunty cozies for your favorite teapots!

FINISHED SIZE

To fit a 4-cup (6-cup) teapot.
Directions given for smaller size; larger size in parentheses ( ).
  Where only one number is given, it applies to both sizes.
15"/38 cm around x 6 (7)"/15 (18) cm tall, measured unstretched.

YARN

Approx. 80 (110) yds/73 (100) m of worsted-weight wool yarn.
We used Rowan *Pure Wool Worsted* (219 yds/200 m); one skein
  should yield two 6-cup cozies.

NEEDLES & NOTIONS

US 6 (4 mm) needles, or size needed to obtain gauge.

2 double-point needles in gauge size for I-cord top.

2 locking markers.

Darning needle to finish.

GAUGE

Approx. 20 sts/36 rows = 4"/10 cm in seed stitch.

GLOSSARY

K = knit; K3Tog = knit 3 stitches together; P = purl; P3Tog = purl 3 stitches together; RS = right side; st(s) = stitch(es); WS = wrong side.

FIRST SIDE

Cast On

Using cable cast-on method, cast on 39 sts.

Welted Edging

Row 1 (WS): Knit.

Row 2 (RS): Purl.

Row 3 (WS): Knit.

NOTE: Purl side of welt will face out, to the RS of cozy.

Next Row (RS): Knit.

Seed Stitch

Work panel in seed stitch as follows:

Row 1 (WS): *K1, P1*; repeat between * * to last st, K1.

Repeat Row 1 30 (38) more times, thus ending with a WS row.

Shape Top

With RS facing, clip markers around base of 11th and 29th sts (both purl sts).

NOTE: Move markers up as you work so you can easily see your marked sts. The marked sts should always be the center of your K3Tog or P3Tog.

Row 1 (RS): *Work in established seed-stitch pattern to 1 st before marked st, P3Tog (then give a little tug to tighten this stitch)*; repeat between * * once more; work in established pattern to end.

Rows 2 & 3: Work in seed-stitch pattern as established.

Row 4 (WS): *Work in seed-stitch pattern to 1 st before marked st, K3Tog (then give a little tug to tighten this stitch)*; repeat between * * once more; work in established pattern to end.

Rows 5 & 6: Work in seed-stitch pattern as established.

Repeat Rows 1–6 two more times. (15 sts)

Next Row (RS): Repeat Row 1. (11 sts)

Next Row (WS): Repeat Row 4. (7 sts)

Next Row (RS): K1, P1, P3Tog, P1, K1. (5 sts)

Cut yarn, leaving an 8"/20 cm tail, and place remaining sts on a double-point needle.

Remove markers and set aside.

SECOND SIDE
Work as for First Side. Do not cut yarn.

I-cord Top
With RS of both pieces facing you, slip Second Side sts onto the double-point needle to the left of the First Side sts.

Turn (WS facing); P2Tog across. (5 sts remain) Turn.

I-cord Row (RS facing): *Knit across; don't turn; slide sts back to right end of needle in left hand, bring yarn across back firmly*. Repeat between * * until cord measures 1"/2.5 cm, or desired length (if you wish to tie a jaunty topknot, you will need at least 4"/10 cm). Cut yarn; with darning needle, thread tail through all sts, draw up tightly and insert tail down through I-cord; trim.

FINISHING

Get your teapot out for a fitting. Mark placement of top and bottom of openings for handle at one side and spout at the other. Using mattress stitch and tails from cast-on, sew seams from bottom edge up to base of handle and spout. Use ending tail from First Side to sew one top seam; use a new piece of yarn to sew second top seam.

Try on teapot to check fit and adjust seams as necessary before weaving in all ends on WS.

Put the kettle on!

what happened in scotland

JANE HAMILTON

*A summer spent living in the Outer Hebrides in 1978 led the
author to turn her back on knitting forever.*

T HIS IS A STORY ABOUT WHY, WHEN I WAS TWENTY, I
turned my back on knitting forever. It wasn't a resolution
or a vow, nothing formal, but rather a deep knowing: I
wasn't going to knit again. It is extremely stupid of me, this stubbornness, because by the accident of fate and the luck of romance
I've lived not only on a farm for over thirty years, but on a farm
with sheep. Every summer when the knitting worsted arrives on
our porch from the mill in Maine, the fleeces of our ordinary,
mutt-variety sheep transformed into yarn in a dazzling array of
color: warm, cool, flecked, heathery, and brash, color you wish
you could somehow ingest, color that should make even the hardest of hearts take up her needles—I am pretty much unmoved. I
should knit, I think, but then I leave the boxes, get the book I'm
dying to finish, and go upstairs to read in that one best place: bed.

The story starts with a handicraft that is not knitting.

In the summer of 1978 I lived in the Outer Hebrides with
Miss Campbell, the last authentic weaver of Harris Tweed. She
dyed the fleeces herself, she spun the wool, she wove on a loom

that was not motorized, she finished the tweeds by a process called waulking, and she sold the fabric in her kitchen, marking off the yards on her table, wrapping the purchase in brown paper, tying it up with string. In Harris Tweed circles she wasn't merely famous, she was a legend. Her customers from the world over sent their requests by mail or trekked to the island to buy that soft wool in exquisitely muted colors. She charged nine pounds a yard, about sixteen dollars.

I was twenty, I'd been studying literature in Edinburgh, and for a reason which now escapes me, I had the idea that I'd like to learn to weave. A friend in the city, a weaver herself, a woman who'd taken the pilgrimage to that kitchen table, suggested I go up to Harris and offer to assist Miss Campbell, that I learn from the master.

At the beginning of July I found the croft, outside of the town of Plocropol, that handful of houses. I knocked on the door, and the legend herself answered, a stout woman with a fleshy pink face, white hair in a bun, an ample bosom, large knobby hands. She was neither happy nor unhappy to see me, neither friendly nor severe. It wasn't unusual for strangers to appear, asking if she needed help, and right there on the stoop she said she'd give me a two-day trial period.

My task for the audition and my primary job for the rest of the summer was to roam the heath and from the granite outcroppings scrape lichens into a bucket. I had a putty knife. The lichens were an essential ingredient for the yellow and green dyes she made. Let me say that those were not the lush, mossy lichens you might find in other parts of the world but Scotch Presbyterian lichens, a gripping, fierce, vegetative dusting holding fast, holding firm. It took most of a day to get half a bucket.

I'd been away from home for over a year then (searching for

my Scotch Presbyterian roots), in an era when there were only those nearly weightless aerograms for news and solace, and there'd been just the one phone call with my parents on Christmas Day. It seemed unlikely that the boy I loved back in Illinois was, after so much time, still true. As I walked from rock to rock along the treeless, windswept shore the seals barked their lonesome *arf arf*; the heather and a variety of grasses were doing their best to take root in the thin soil—the hillocks themselves, the gentle swells of earth, the very ground seemed lonesome; the sky was pale, and often white and empty; the white beach deserted, the landscape, all of it, aching for everything that was missing. Have I said that I was just twenty? That gorgeous desolation was set in place, it seemed, to intensify the isolation and homesickness I'd felt all year at the university.

Miss Campbell had lived most of her adult life alone in that small croft but in the last several years her brother, who was then in his nineties, had come to stay. As I remember her story she'd learned her craft from an aunt. She'd shown early promise and when she was about my age she'd won the Harris Tweed Association Design Competition, beating out older established weavers on the island. The techniques were handed down in the family, generation to generation, but the job was a calling, a life as austere as taking religious orders. If she was going to weave, she'd once told me, if that was the choice she was to make at the age of eighteen, then she would not marry. For over fifty years she'd worked six days a week, a devotion that confined her and within the limits of that art set her free.

As for travel, there had been one trip off the island. She'd gone to London because she'd been granted an audience with the queen. The photograph of the occasion was on a shelf in the living room, the two smiling women with vastly different experiences, and yet in their commitment to duty and their discovery of self through work they might well have been soul sisters. In 1985, several years after I'd lived with her, when she was awarded the British Empire Medal, she declined another trip to Buckingham Palace, declaring that the medal was not for her but for the Isle of Harris.

After I passed the lichen-scraping test I was told to pack up my tent at the nearby campground and move my things to the upstairs bedroom of the croft. Although Miss Campbell knew almost nothing about me she'd determined that I was strong and hardworking and quiet, and so could sleep in her house, in the room under the eaves, with the dormer windows that looked out to the sea. It was cold but romantic—I did know that any onlooker would think that.

There were four of us in the household, Miss Campbell, her aged brother, and their visiting nephew, who was in his early thirties, and during the year taught high school. He'd come from Glasgow to help his uncle dig the peats, which was the source of heat for the house. Was he merely shy, I wonder now, or was he depressed, or was he actually as hostile as he looked? Certainly he was cheerless, a brawny man with wavy dark hair, and sharply drawn sideburns practically to his jaw, the quiet type, the suspect you'd think of first after a murder in the neighborhood. At breakfast and lunch and dinner, with our plates before us of oatcakes and whatever else we had with that staple, fish and boiled cabbage, or cheese, there was almost no conversation. I don't know if my presence inhibited them, or if through the years they had exhausted all their material, or if the work we were doing had numbed our minds, or if their gene pool—our gene pool, had produced naturally taciturn peoples, the Outer Hebridean breed the prizewinners. For whatever reason from Monday through Saturday we ate in silence. On Sunday, their day of rest, of more silence, I supposed, or reading the Bible, I was given a wax paper bag of oat-cakes and cheese and instructed not to come back until evening. That day of rest was a trial for Miss Campbell because when she could not work she did not sleep well.

There was a television in the living room and a radio, but I don't remember either of them ever being used. In the evenings, after teatime, we sat. The uncle and nephew sat on the sofa beneath the large picture window that looked out to the sea, and Miss Campbell sat across from them in a high-backed padded chair that didn't recline, the Scotch Presbyterian version of the La-Z-Boy. I sat on a little sofa next to her. Soon after we'd taken our places the uncle fell asleep, his thin-lipped, toothless mouth hanging open, that great, sad, gaping hole, the rattly breathing. The nephew took several weeks to read *To Kill a Mockingbird*. Miss Campbell knit. The first night of this routine, when I'd opened my book, she shooed it away. "No, no, no, girrrl!" That was what she called me, and probably every young woman who came to scrape lichens. "No reading!" she ordered. "No book!"

The nephew was allowed to read because his work required it, or maybe because he was a man he could do as he liked. To her way of thinking, though, reading must have seemed a frippery. I realize now that she may well have been illiterate, or she read only the Bible in Gaelic. She clearly felt a deep sense of exclusion in the presence of a reader of novels. What was I to do then, I wondered to myself, if not read? She asked me if I knew how to knit, and I said yes. My grandmother had taught me years before but it was not something I'd ever taken up in earnest. Miss Campbell gave me a ball of store-bought yarn, and told me to make a scarf, sensing, no doubt, that anything more complicated was beyond my reach.

I'd never been cut off from the thing I most needed, a novel to read, to set myself into, that singular pleasure, the mystical companionship of a writer's mind. I needed not only that company but the music of language, the texture and song of speech, what was so absent during my days on the heath and at the table and at night in the living room. I often felt like crying. And yet it was wrong, I knew, to despair during this experience that so many people, real weavers, would die for, this time wasted on me, an ingrate who no longer wanted to be involved with handicrafts of any kind.

My scarf was a shapeless nothing, every stitch a marker of time, the clock on the wall with its loud ticking, the seconds of those long northern sunlit nights slowly passing. I thought as I knit about how Miss Campbell's life had not always been silent; surely it had not always been so. When she was a girl the weavers had worked communally, gathering in the waulking shed to rhythmically beat the tweed on a board, the technique to shrink the fabric, the women in that enclosed society singing the age-old ballads as they passed the tweed from hand to hand. That era and that community were gone forever, now only the two of us in the shed, the songs playing in her head perhaps, songs that I had read about at the School of Scottish Studies in Edinburgh, songs that, if I'd been a bold person I would have asked her to sing, or to teach me.

I thought about the things I might have done if I hadn't felt so blank or been so timid, my uneven knit-purl, knit-purl, the scarf—if you could call it that—something I would later stuff into a wastebasket in a bathroom at the Glasgow airport on my way home, a thing so alarming that probably in this day and age TSA would shut the place down, fearful of a bomb in that webby mass.

The summer was not without its excitements, Miss Campbell anxiously preparing for the annual fair in Tarbet, where she swept up the blue ribbons, as she always did, taking the first prizes for her tweeds. One day my mother arrived, our plans made only via those aerograms, my joyous, loud, Midwestern mother unexpected on that afternoon, doing a jig of happiness in the narrow hall of the croft, surely blowing the minds of the Campbells. I did understand that I would never again be as lonely, that the crushing silence of that house was probably going to be a once-in-a-lifetime experience. I knew, certainly, that I would get back to a place where I could read, and that I would never take for granted the miracle that is a novel. Which is why—even now, when I look at that other miracle, the knitting worsted that arrives in box after box from Maine on our doorstep—why I admire the wool, I smell it, I sink my hands into it, but then head upstairs, get my book from the night table, and begin to read.

my mother-in-law, her knitting, and me

CATHI HANAUER

*How a heather blue sweater became the conduit to the
author's understanding of family.*

THE FIRST GIFT MY MOTHER-IN-LAW GAVE ME—
twenty-three years ago, a year after I met her son and my
soon-to-be husband, Dan—was a heather blue crew-neck
wool sweater, with a cable yoke, that she'd knit. Dan and I lived
in Tucson, Arizona, but we had come back east for winter break,
and I needed warm things to wear. We were spending Christmas
with his parents in Virginia, in their cozy cabin in a ski resort in
the Blue Ridge Mountains. Their regular home was in Wisconsin,
where Dan's father, Chuck, taught political science. He was born
in South Dakota, and Dan's mother, Vera, in Vienna, Austria,
and when the temperature went above, say, 35, they needed to
get somewhere colder, fast—preferably straight onto a ski slope.
(Vera's father, who was almost ninety at the time, had stopped
downhill skiing just a year or two before.)

The sweater was beautiful, comfortable, and warm; it fit perfectly, and it looked country-cool with jeans and boots. But that

was the least of it. Being presented with this hand-made gift by my future mother-in-law was one more sign that she, like her son, saw me as someone worthy of becoming part of their family. And in fact, when I put it on, I happily felt myself almost physically transformed from my old self, and life, into "someone like them"— specifically, what I saw as a combination of classy WASPyness (their name was Jones, after all, even if Vera was actually half Catholic and half Jewish) and down-home, hearty, Good Country Folk, leading a Heidi-esque lifestyle of mountains and woodstoves, rosy cheeks and homemade granola, worn work boots and, well, hand-knit sweaters.

This, I felt, was pretty much the opposite of who I was and what I'd been. It wasn't that no one in my family ever knit—my maternal grandmother crocheted, and my paternal was actually quite skilled with needles and yarn—or that my family wasn't also creative and down-home in a certain way. My mother, besides being a skilled cook and gardener, was no slouch at her Singer, and in my childhood she'd whipped off, for my sisters and me, everything from matching "maxi" skirts (for a wedding) to matching clown costumes (Halloween). But in general, my parents were bookish, hyper, theater-going Jews from suburban New Jersey, Dad a bossy, often volatile physician, and Mom, after a decade-plus hiatus to raise her four children, a bustling teacher of the physically handicapped. They didn't ski—too cold, too dangerous—and in the winter, they went somewhere warm (think Club Med), where they could read books (Mom), play tennis (Dad), and swim in a pool or the balmy Caribbean Sea.

I too, of course, was manic and bossy, played tennis, read too much, and had always preferred a heated, chlorine-scented pool to an icy ski slope. What's more, I had been raised in a town that—at least in retrospect—seemed the antithesis of knitting. Growing up in *Sopranos*-esque West Orange, New Jersey, in the late seventies (think *Saturday Night Fever*), I was surrounded by tiny, curvy Italian girls with big hair and bigger shoes and boys named Anthony, Mario, and Vinnie. My best friend's father, whom I'll call Mr. Zeferelli, was a bookie, and at times when I was at the Zeferelli house, which was pretty much whenever I wasn't sleeping (and sometimes when I was), we had to hide with the lights off when a black Cadillac pulled up and three men in suits sauntered up the front walk to ring the bell. The Zeferelli girls—five if you included their blue-eyed, D-cupped mother—wore their hair long, their jeans tight, their shoes spiked, and their eyelashes Clairol-enhanced or fake, and there was never a time, day or night, when the jumbo hot rollers weren't plugged in. Jackets, when worn at all, were leather or imitation rabbit, short and tight and usually white, zipped to half-mast for full cleavage display.

Since I loved and idolized the Zeferellis and their home—disco boomed from the eight-track, meatballs sizzled on the stove, someone was always dancing or making out with a boy on the couch or buying press-on nails, mood rings, or hair-frosting kits in a box from the shopping channel on TV—I tried my best to dress like them, and I probably don't need to say that homemade crew-neck wool sweaters weren't exactly the rage. I kept up their extreme New Jersey style through college, teetering around the deep snow of Syracuse University in fur-lined spike clogs (perfect for icy sidewalks; they pierced down and stuck, anchoring me) and tiny suede jackets, minus scarves, hats, or, really, anything remotely warm. I honestly don't know how I didn't freeze to death there.

After Syracuse, I went to New York City, where I still tended toward "fashion" extremes, i.e., nothing even vaguely practical, let alone homemade. For my first day of my first real-world job—as an intern at *Seventeen* magazine—I wore a pink polka-dot micro-minidress with cotton-candy-colored pumps. (Thankfully, my boss—a Southern former sorority girl who loved theater—found me amusing instead of appalling.) If I wore a sweater at all—which I did now and then in the winter—it tended toward low-cut, store-bought, and machine-made, in colors and material resembling nothing in nature: neon acrylics, polyester with metallic streaks. It wasn't until almost a decade later, when I met Dan and headed off to join him at graduate school in Tucson, that I learned the alternate appeal of air-dried hair, no makeup, loose jeans, and flat shoes—partly because that's all I could afford in those years, and partly because, as a creative writing grad student in the desert, rocking Sergio Valenti flares and five-inch Lucite heels would have made me a freak.

The point is, for the first three decades of my life I was not a person who wore thick home-knit crew-neck sweaters. Until I met Dan and his family. Dan Jones, to be exact. I blinked at the simplicity of even his name. He was tall (tall! as opposed to short, wide, and V-shaped) and calm and wore work boots and soft faded jeans—Levi's, not Calvin or Jordache or Valenti—and loose-fitting cotton shirts. No extra-large, gold-plated crucifix rings (I had given my main high school squeeze, Serafino, one for some birthday, and he'd worn it faithfully), no chains dripping down his exposed hairy chest. Dan didn't lift weights or play football or go to the gym (though he did bike and run and play Ultimate). He had one sibling, not four or six, and had grown up in big old houses with drafty windows and fireplaces and rolling green hills, or quiet snowy woods, right outside. When his father wasn't preparing for a class, writing a book, delivering a lecture, or speaking at an event, he worked outside moving rocks or clearing snow and ice, or inside repairing stuff with the antique tools he collected. Chuck was careful and polite, distinguished and handy. And

Vera—sunny, warm, intelligent, and (like Dan) a little bit shy—
was his faithful, loving, and beloved wife, who not only kept house
and cooked meals and met everyone's considerable needs, but also
almost always was knitting something.

I loved the Joneses—maybe even as much as I'd once loved
the Zeferellis. And I was ready for something different, and with
this family, as proven with this beautiful homemade sweater, I felt
I'd found it. Vera was disciplined and efficient in the same ways as
my own mother (and as so many middle-class wives of that generation). But she also had a certain calm that my own high-energy,
high-achieving family seemed to lack, and that, by extension,
I did too. Like my mother, Vera made delicious chocolate des-
serts, but unlike my mother, she actually sat down and ate them
("I shouldn't," she'd say, happily popping a square of fudge in her
mouth), while my mother's enjoyment came from watching others
indulge in her handiwork. My mother—a woman who, like me,
weighs 90 pounds soaking wet—went to bed late (still does), got
up early (ditto), and seemed to devour books all night long (she
belongs to two book clubs and reads "on the side" in between), and
even now, at seventy-eight, rarely sits, except to quickly down a
slice-of-cheese-on-toast-with-black-coffee lunch or to watch *Masterpiece Theatre* with my father when he makes her. Vera, in con-
trast, will happily collapse on the couch at the end of a long day to
watch a chick flick by choice. But then, Vera has her knitting.

It took both learning her rather amazing history and observing
her over more than two decades for me to realize how much of
Vera's personality—her generosity, her passion, her joie de vivre,
and even to some extent her healthy stubbornness—is reflected in
her knitting; I also came to realize I might not be as different from
her as I'd thought, though our histories could not be more different. Vera was born in Vienna, in 1935—to a Catholic mother

(Ann) and a Jewish father (Joe)—and by the time she was three, the Holocaust and World War II were beginning, and they knew that Joe needed to leave. He was working as a lawyer in the Austrian Chamber of Labour, but when the Nazis took over, he was fired for being Jewish and told he had to vacate their (government-owned) apartment within two weeks. The family moved into Ann's parents' home as the situation worsened; soon Joe had to wear a Jewish star and to bike everywhere, forbidden to take public transportation. He planned to leave in July—he would escape by walking over the mountains to Switzerland, à la the von Trapp family—but just about that time, he got an invitation to go to England and teach at the Labour College at Oxford (he also had a PhD), and that allowed him to get a visa from the British embassy and leave safely. He left in July, and Ann and Vera followed in September, though they almost didn't get out: a Swiss guard on the train stopped them, suspecting they were fleeing, but then he saw Vera sleeping, smiled (she was an adorable child), and let them go. I often think that if it weren't for the kindness of that guard, my husband and children would not exist.

In England, Joe taught German at Oxford. For extra income, Ann took on sewing, something she'd been trained in at a young age. As a girl from a struggling family in Vienna, she had not been allowed to go to school beyond eighth grade or to take music lessons; she cared for her two younger brothers in the afternoons while her parents worked, and, upon graduating what we would call middle school, she entered a profession: sewing. After her training, she went to work sewing for a company. But she also joined the Socialist Youth Movement, and that's where, eventually, she met Joe. When they married—she was twenty-five, he twenty-nine—she was able to give up her job, though she still sewed, including Vera's and her own clothes.

But in England—where Joe could no longer practice law, not having been trained in that country—Ann went back to work. Vera remembers, as a three-year-old, being brought along to people's houses where her mother had sewing or alteration jobs, and being expected to sit quietly on the floor, sometimes for hours, as her mother worked and people spoke English around her (frustrating for her, as she had just been learning to talk—but in German, the language of Austria—when they left). Two years later, they came to the U.S., first to New York, where they lived with other refugees in a big house with a shared kitchen and Vera attended nursery school as her mother worked for the Austrian clothier Lanz, then to Washington, D.C., and then, two years later, to Madison, Wisconsin, where Joe could work in the field of labor education once again, and Ann could quit work, raise Vera, and again sew purely for pleasure or charity. Which she did, making everything from curtains for the minister's wife at the Unitarian church she and Joe attended to, eventually, Vera's wedding dress.

Vera grew up watching her mother sew and knit, and soon enough she learned, too. But she was never the seamstress her mother was—Ann was an artist, who could envision a dress on a person and then make it to fit without the person having to try it on; who could make a worn man's suit into a beautiful women's suit during wartime, when material was scarce—and Vera soon came to prefer knitting: the pretty yarns and colors, the fact that you could rip it out and start over if it didn't come out the way you wanted. Her mother taught her to knit "the European way"—yarn in the left hand—though now she does both: convenient when she's making something with two colors, as she can knit the main color the European way, then "carry the other color and throw it over like Americans do." ("So if the base is red and I want to put in some white," she explains, "I can make the stitch quickly knitting the European way and then put in the colors the American way.")

Despite other passions as a teenager—skiing, riding horses—Vera kept knitting, if casually. She particularly liked clicking away cold winter evenings in Wisconsin: the relaxing rhythm of the needles, the feel of the soft yarn against her hands. She found it soothing—maybe, she imagines, not so different from how smoking must feel like for a smoker. She liked having something to do with her hands when watching TV or talking to someone, liked watching patterns unfold. Norwegian patterns were a favorite, especially on mittens, scarves, and hats. At Carleton, where she first went to college, she volunteered to knit a very long stocking cap as a funny class gift for the president at an event; it had six feet of patterned "tail" that crossed around (and around) his neck, with a fluffy ball on the end. Everyone loved it.

A year or two later, after transferring back to the U of Wisconsin, she was offered a job at a yarn store in Madison; they knew her from coming in to buy yarn and sometimes returning with the projects to ask a question. The store was owned by a mother and daughter who also were artists in a sense: they could design a sweater, print up the pattern, and tell you how much yarn to buy. Vera learned quickly from them. She also got discounts on yarns. All fueled her knitting enthusiasm.

In many ways, Vera's passion for and mastery of knitting was not unlike mine for writing: some was innate and some learned; some a hobby (or, in my case, a career), and some a thing she did because she craved it. And much of it was no doubt fueled by positive feedback from friends, family, strangers, and people like, say, me, whose experience with knitting consists of once attempting a "blanket" that I abandoned when it was cocktail-napkin-sized and looked like something the cat dragged in. Vera talks with confidence about knitting in a way I rarely hear her talk about anything else—not her cooking (which is delicious), her dogs (who are always impeccably trained), or her (considerable) intelligence or beauty. She's a humble, sometimes even insecure person, but about her knitting, she can say, more matter-of-factly than boastfully, "I know few people who knit better than I do."

She likes when people bring her their knitting problems and she can solve them. And she likes to knit gifts—complicated aran-pattered afghans for her children, tiny sweaters when her grandchildren were babies, layettes for charity: a blanket with a matching sweater and hat. About a dozen years ago, her two granddaughters—one of them my daughter, Phoebe—began collecting American Girl dolls. Vera took one look at the catalog of clothes (and the hefty price tags) and thought, "I can do that." Soon after, she found a store that sold the patterns, and she went to work, knitting a gorgeous mohair cardigan with beautiful, fancy buttons—one doll-sized, one human girl-sized. Pink, variegated, with shades of violet and red and purple. Phoebe got one and her doll got the other, and both fit perfectly. Later, she made dozens more doll outfits, both for Phoebe and her cousin, and for a local charity—each with a fancy sweater, knitted "jeans," and a hat—and raised hundreds of dollars for them. But she got bored with that after a while, and moved on to other things. More gorgeous sweaters, elegant black angora scarves and cowls, wool socks, mohair mittens. Our dogs—mutts literally rescued off the streets of Puerto Rico—got exquisite handmade coats, multicolored blankets of stripes made using "all my old scraps of yarn"—fifty or sixty stripes in each, gray and cobalt with streaks of red, sky blue, lemon, even some pink. Their names—Rosie and Rico—are knit perfectly into the neck. People stop us on the streets to ask about those jackets.

When I suggest, as I have, that Vera take orders and charge for her projects—because I'd need many hands to count the number of people even I know who would pay good money for them—she shakes her head. Though she's happy to donate her work, she has no interest in doing it as more than just a pastime. For a long time, I didn't understand that. Why, my thinking went, would someone want to "live off her husband," taking care of him and his household while he earned all the money and got all the prestige? But now, in midlife myself (as she was when I met her), I get it. Vera didn't want to knit when she wasn't inspired, and she didn't want to have to worry about getting it perfect. She wanted the freedom to be able to rip it out if she didn't like it (and in fact, she still claims she's as happy to redo a project-gone-wrong than to start a new one, since much of what she loves is the process), and she didn't want to have to worry about pleasing others to the exclusion, perhaps, of herself. And why should she? My father-in-law has worked hard and been very successful, in no small part because of Vera's support of his career. And his success is hers too, and she is grateful to have what she wants and needs. She feels lucky and happy.

And I think that's part of what I first saw in Vera, and relished in the very first sweater she made me—that genuine happiness. What took me a little longer to get was that her cheerfulness about living for her husband and family, about being able to knit what she wants when she wants to and gift it to people or to charity, about running a household right down to sewing and knitting its clothes, felt as much like a privilege to her as having a career did to me. For both of us, it was a ticket to following our passion and serving those we love while maintaining a certain autonomy.

These days, Vera's into the Japanese Noro yarn, with its intense colors and natural fiber feel; for her seventy-eighth birthday, she requested enough yarn to knit a three-quarters length sweater for herself, which of course turned out stunning: triangular splashes of vivid colors, mostly reds and maroons. She's in heaven working with those beautiful yarns and patterns. As for me, I'm pretty content these days too, though admittedly I've still yet to take up knitting. And while I like to think that I've picked up some of the Joneses' calm and country class, the truth is, I'm a combination of my parents, my childhood hometown, and the family I married into, not to mention the family Dan and I have created: two kids and two dogs in a Victorian house in (yes) snowy New England. I still prefer high heels to flats, long hair to short, and a good book to a ski slope. But I also still have that heather blue sweater. And sometimes—especially on biting winter days—I put it on, and it still keeps me as warm as the day Vera gave it to me.

the italian hat

LILY KING

*A knitted hat keeps the author's daughter warm
during their year in Italy.*

PICTURE US: FATHER, MOTHER, AND TWO YOUNG
daughters walking single-file with groceries up the narrow
sidewalk in San Casciano Val di Pesa, singing show tunes.

I know I mustn't fall into the pit,
But when I'm with a feller, I fergit!

Right now it's *Oklahoma!* we're obsessed with. Our girls are at that
precious age, six and eight, when they are not yet embarrassed
to sing in the street, not yet embarrassed that their parents are
singing in the street, and not yet conscious of the stereotype of
the loud American in Europe or that we are reinforcing it. They
still wear pigtails and sundresses. Eloise, the younger one, carries
a large deer with stiff legs called Deerie most places. Calla stops
to smell all the flowers, so many of them snaking up the old walls
around the town, bursting out from between the stones.

We have just arrived in Italy, but we are not tourists. We have
a year's lease on a tiny apartment inside a fourteenth-century bish-

op's castle at the top of the hill. San Casciano (San Cash, we will start calling it soon, both because *s* and *c* together in Italian make the *sh* sound and because as time goes on and the dollar—it is 2007—starts to plummet, our savings disappear faster and faster) holds the same number of people as our small town in Maine. But unlike our town, whose main street has few stores and fewer pedestrians, the *centro* of this village is stuffed with shops and restaurants—over seventy storefronts on four short streets—and people. Midmorning, high noon, late afternoon, and long into the evening, the town is always crowded: old men in their requisite fishing vests (though they are not fishing); old women with their hair all dyed the same ruddy auburn; teenagers smoking and making out (our girls cannot take their eyes away), young parents in suits or heels or both, their children fighting over packets of Ringos. They gather inside at Caffè Vittorio, Ristorante Nonno, and Bar Turismo, and they gather outside in the *piazza dell'orologio*, on the benches set against the old walls, and, beyond the walls, in the park they call the *piazzone*.

At first we know no one but our landlady Marisa and her husband Mauro. Mauro is a magician who used to own the toy shop next to the jeweler's, but he retired, sold the business, and now gives magic classes in the little office above his old store. Marisa greets us with the keys the day we arrive, leads us down the path from the gate at the street that runs through the old bishop's olive trees to the little castle everyone in town calls the *cassero*. Our apartment is at the side on the right, a small patio out front with green plastic furniture and a rack for drying clothes. After she pushes open the enormous door, she tells us many, many things, some of which I understand. I've been taking Italian lessons; Tyler has not. Marisa quickly and permanently dismisses him, never speaking directly to him again, always pointing and referring to him, like most Italians, as Taylor. *Taylor non capisce!* She doubles over laughing. It's her favorite joke, one that never gets old.

For the two weeks before the girls' school starts, we take our summer vacation. We explore our town and others nearby. We go up to Firenze and down to San Gimignano. We stay on American time, sleeping in and staying up late, which conveniently puts us on Italian time. But really, we eat. We eat familiar dishes like *prosciutto e melone*, *insalata caprese*, and *pasta al pesto*, and we eat new things like *fiori di zucca fritti* (fried zucchini flowers), *pici al tartuffo* (a thick spaghetti with truffles), and *penne strascicate* (penne with a meat sauce).

The food is not good simply because Italians know how to cook, how to combine ingredients to perfection. It's the ingredients themselves. The flavors of even the most basic foods here are on steroids. They make you feel like you have been eating cardboard until this moment. There is no way to overstate this. The tomatoes, the grapes, the melon, the figs—we in the States eat shadows of these foods, as if a set designer has stocked our grocery stores with realistic-looking produce for a play. There are many theories about this: the ash in the soil, the local sourcing, the reverence of taste above all else, above even making a profit (an unthinkable scrambling of American values). Our kids notice the difference. Once picky eaters, they now eat everything, try everything, begin to feel passionate about the *raviolini melanzane* from the pasta shop, the butcher's *ragù*, and the *paste crema* at the Turismo.

In the afternoons we take our rental car into the hills, and in the evenings we watch those same hills from the *piazzone* while the girls race around the enormous play castle. We eat gelato as the sun sinks beyond the ripples of rows of grape and olive trees, the spears of cypress, the burnt red roofs of villas and farmhouses and bell towers, a great gorgeous smear of earth's colors deepened by the sun's last shafts. The light here tastes as good as the food it grows.

WE ARE, I PROMISE, GETTING TO THE KNITTING.

The girls' school is in a smaller village called La Romola. To get there means a harrowing fifteen-minute drive through the hills on roads that are more like thinly paved paths. It means sucking in your breath when a bus comes around a hairpin turn straight for you and you know for a fact that your vehicle and that bigger vehicle cannot both fit in the width of this road, that one of you will be thwumped off the edge into the vineyards below, then within seconds (because the speed of the oncoming traffic is as terrifying as the spatial dynamics) the bus is behind you and maybe your side mirror has been knocked in but otherwise you are unscathed. The last hill is basically vertical and you are surprised each time your rental car does not do a back flip.

It is a small school, one story, six rooms, a former *caserma dei carabinieri*, a police station, but an elegant one, with French doors in front and tall windows with green shutters, elaborate ironwork all around it. It's private but cheap by American standards, about a thousand euros each. We felt the children might get lost at the large regional school in San Cash, so we chose this one which goes from grades one to five, no more than nine kids in a class.

To school each day they must bring a *pentolino*, a small metal container with a lid and a handle and the child's name written in permanent marker, filled with their pasta lunch. When the students arrive at school they all place their *pentolini* in a large vat with a few inches of water on the bottom. Midmorning Ludovica, the school's assistant, will press a button and the water will heat up and all the pasta lunches will be warm by noon.

It is as strange for us as for the children, walking into school that first day, all the parents and children talking at lightning speed. There is a brief ceremony in the room of *la quarta*, fourth grade. A few teachers speak. One seems to be new, replacing someone who is sick. The older children sing, very loudly. Then we break up and take the kids to their classrooms. Up to now, Calla has been stoic, but at the door to her third grade classroom she clutches my fingers and I can't free them. When she cries red welts form under her eyes. The other children pass through. She is the last one. I tell her she can do this, that it will never be this hard again. Her teacher, Elena, comes over and speaks to her gently with bits of English. Calla nods and looks into the room. It is noisy and chaotic; two boys are wrestling and knocking around the desks. They are all speaking so fast. Her face is bright red and wet. She looks at me and laughs at the absurdity of having to spend a day, let alone a whole school year, in there. She grips my fingers tighter, then lets go.

Eloise is next. Her teacher, Neri, has a beard, ponytail, and a lip piercing, and I think the fact that he is a man is harder for her than the fact that he, unlike Elena, does not speak a word of English. Eloise won't go in the classroom without us, so Neri tells us we can stay for the first few minutes. We sit on the floor just behind her chair in the circle while he tells them a story, something about a girl collecting one kind of flower and a boy collecting another and one of the bunches of flowers smelled good. But I can't concentrate on the story. I'm only thinking about how we are going to leave this room without Eloise following us. There is a moral to the story, something about how you never know what you are going to need later in life, I think, but I don't know how it connects to the bunches of flowers. Then desks are pulled out from against the wall and Neri seats the students in pairs. Eloise sits with a girl named Daria, Ludovica's daughter. Daria is talking to her and she is listening or pretending to listen. We stand and she gives us a brief look—*you still here?*—before we walk out.

We are the last to leave, the odd Americans in their odd clothing (I in my comfortable sandals, Tyler in a baseball cap, no doubt), out through the big doors and across the playground to the road. We walk past our car. The land to our left swells in steep waves all the way back to San Casciano, a mist still languishing in the valleys. I can't appreciate the beauty right now, so I resent it trailing beside me. We make a short loop down and around town, which consists of one bar and one tractor repair shop. We walk back up to the school. The windows of Calla's classroom are open and we stop and listen. They are singing.

Tyler and I get in the car and drive back home. We are both writers and are supposed to be getting back to work ourselves. Instead, we worry. We know it cannot be going well. How could it be going well? At lunch in the *piazza dell'orologio* we try to prepare our response to the girls when they tell us on the way home from school that they are never ever going back to that school again. Tyler comes up with our surest defense: It's the law. That's what we will tell them. It's the law that children go to school and we live here now and this is where you must go to school. And I like that, because they are very into the law and not going to jail.

But when we go back at two, Calla hugs us and says she loves school. Eloise and Daria come running up and grab us by the hands. *Venite,* Daria says, *venite vedere le case di gnomi che abbiamo fatto.* And we all go look at the gnome houses they made. She and Daria climb up the tree their little house is built into. I burst into tears of relief.

The year is that easy for Eloise. By the end of the first week I can hear her speaking on the playground: *vieni qui* or *dai* or, as we are leaving, *a domani!* Daria takes her firmly under her wing, and what Eloise cannot say Daria says for her.

But Calla does not have a Daria. The two other girls in her class do not take her on as their personal responsibility. Sofia is a tomboy who only wants to play with the boys and Anita is too shy at first to befriend anyone. A few of the boys pick on Anita, which drives her further into herself. Calla is on her own, except at recess when she plays with other girls from other grades who speak some English: half-American Esmeralda, half-English Isabelle, and quarter-English Carolina. But in her classroom, she remains the silent girl. They call her La Calla affectionately, but she does not speak. She is listening, though. She brings home words and phrases—*ganzo, ci vuole, c'è l'ho*—and we pore over the dictionary together, piecing the language together, separating standard expressions from slang, Italian from regional dialect. When we go to buy a tablecloth and napkins we practice together outside the shop how to ask for them, but I am the one who will speak them. She won't speak Italian in public. She is hoarding her words, saving them up for when they can spill out of her mouth correctly and in the right order.

I take Calla to Sofia's birthday party. They play a game where someone gets blindfolded and has to search around with a stick for a big pot with a present in it while everyone else calls out *Aqua!* if the person is moving away from the pot and *Fuoco!* if the person is moving towards it. Calla doesn't play. Cutting off another sense does not appeal to her. Sofia's mother doesn't introduce me to the other parents. I smile and they smile but they do not introduce themselves. Soon I learn to do it myself, learn that people in these small towns are not in the habit of introducing anyone because they have all known each other all their lives; they are happy to let a *straniera* remain a *straniera*. Later, I watch Calla play a memory game with Sofia and Anita. It's a long game with so many cards, all of which seem to be dinosaurs. Calla makes strange noises instead of speaking. When the game is finally over and we can go home, Calla whispers in my ear, "You gotta be a little more standoffish / When fellers offer you a buggy ride." Lines from *Oklahoma!* The music, I think, must have been comforting her the whole day.

The two classes Calla loves are English and handwork. English is where she gets a bit of her power back. When they play store, she knows how to ask for any item imaginable. She knows how to add up the merchandise—she knows the word merchandise. It is the one time of day when she blooms, when her classmates hear her voice.

Handwork is taught as part of the school's philosophy of nurturing the head, hands, and heart of each child. But for eight-year-olds, it is also a race. And Calla, undistracted by the chatter, is fast. The handwork projects stay at school, in a little basket they can pull out only during handwork class. First they sew pouches for their needles. She finishes first and is given an extra project until everyone else has caught up. Next they make the knitting needles. They whittle one end and put a ball of wax at the other so the stitches don't fall off. Then the handwork *maestra* teaches them how to knit a hat. Calla has been knitting since kindergarten. She is very fast.

By now it is late fall. Eloise speaks in fragments with her friends. And Calla is still the silent girl. Her school days have highs and lows. One day she sees a boy named Gioele point to her polka-dot corduroys and snicker with Ricardo. She comes home and tells me about it. The place under her eyes grows red as she speaks. She only has a few pairs of pants here and those are her favorite. She does not wear them the next day, or the next. But they are back in rotation by the end of the week.

One of their class projects that fall is a big Nativity scene made out of beeswax to be displayed at a community hospital in December. They start with the trees. Calla shows me her tree after school one day. All the trees are standing straight up except the one she points to, which is bent over as if in a storm. Listening to Italian all day, I think, is a big wind. A few weeks later she gets assigned the baby Jesus. Sofia is assigned Mary, and this bonds them a bit. One day at lunchtime Sofia fetches Calla's *pentolino* for her. Calla tells me that night that she feels she should do the same for Sofia the next day but she's not sure which is hers. She says that Gioele is a nice boy (unlike me, she has forgiven Gioele for the pants insult) and that he sometimes brings everyone's *pentolini* into the classroom for them. "Even mine," she says. The "even mine" breaks my heart a little.

No one ever tells you about the winter in Italy. In all the travel logs and memoirs, the books about renting villas and renovating farmhouses, apprenticing as a chef, a butcher, a vintner, everything seems to take place between April and October. In those books, it is always spring, summer, or fall. As if winter did not exist in Italy.

The winter we were in San Cash it rained. It rained and rained. It snowed a few times, brief overnight dustings that melted underfoot and were gone by midmorning. But the rest of the time it rained, a cold rain that seeped into the stone of our castle and every other building in town like it seeped into our bones. A rain just short of frozen, the kind of wet cold no Italian coat or American parka can protect you from.

At the beginning of this season, the wet stone and bone season, Calla comes home with her hat. It is striped, six different colors. The band around the forehead has a different stitch than the rest, a looser, watery stitch. The wool is rough, fresh, and smells like a barn. The colors are like looking out at the hills from our park at sunset, the rust red of the rooftops and the light green of the *olivi* and the dark green of the cypress, the blue of the fading sky, the yellow and peach of the sinking sun. The rows are straight and even. The half-finished scarf I keep under the bed is full of holes and clumps, but Calla's hat has no mistakes.

She comes out of school with the hat on her head, weeks before anyone else finishes theirs, and it doesn't come off. She wears it every day to school. She wears it on the field trip to the hospital where their beeswax Nativity scene is on display with many others, some made of pasta, some of beans. She wears it when our friends Lucy and Riccardo take us to the *presepe vivente* in Castelfranco, where real people, dressed up as Mary and Joseph, shepherds and kings, act out the Holy Night, and where, in the middle of the fake manger, there is a real baby in the cradle. She wears it to Sestri Levante where we celebrate New Year's with our new Norwegian friends, and to Siena, and to Assisi.

By the time the hat comes off, sometime in late February, when the sky has cleared and the sun has remembered Italy, La Calla has begun speaking Italian. Gorgeously, in long grammatically correct sentences. In the past. In the future. With slang I do not understand.

For her birthday in March she has a sleepover, seven friends, from second grade through fifth. We have an egg and spoon race, eat dinner and cake, and when they are all squeezed into sleeping bags up in the girls' tiny loft, Tyler performs a magic show. He has been taking classes with Mauro. He makes a wand rise and fall from a wine bottle; he has them play a shell game with matchboxes; he wraps a rope around his neck twice, knots it, then with one tug the rope snaps magically off his neck, all in one piece. I take videos and later I can't pick out my children from the Italian voices in the background.

In the spring *la terza* starts rehearsing a *recita*, a play, about Isacco and Abramo. Yes, I think it is a disturbing and inappropriate subject for eight-year-olds, but I have few standards left. We have allowed our children to squeeze with many others into Italian cars without seatbelts, shown them all the hideously gory Renaissance deaths and beheadings in museums and churches, and, having rented every G and PG film at Ugo's closet-sized video store, have moved on to the PG-13s. Calla is Abramo's bewildered wife whose husband wants to kill their child to prove his loyalty to God. She has memorized not just her lines, mostly to her servant who acts as her therapist, but every line of the play. At night in our *cassero*, she acts the whole thing out in fast, fluid Italian, flawless as her hat.

THAT HAT, WHICH once covered her ears and skimmed her eyebrows, now barely fits on Calla's fifteen-year-old head. She has lost most of her Italian, as we all have, a sad, *Flowers for Algernon*–like vanishing of knowledge. But she is quite passionate about language, Latin and French these days.

I touch the hat. It is still coarse, the colors still luminous.

Picture her, La Calla, in her polka-dot pants in the classroom of an old *carabinieri* station, listening, straining, absorbing—each word a stitch and the stitches growing into rows, the language and the hat taking shape all at once in her hands, her head, and her heart. Picture her, knitting like the wind.

the museum of the lady with only one neck

PERRI KLASS

*The author embarks on the heartbreaking task of emptying
her mother's apartment and in so doing reclaims
what she'd knit for her.*

I. WHAT IS LOST: *the gray Icelandic sweater*

My great guilty secrets as a knitter are related: I am almost always
warm when I am inside, and I do not comfortably wear wool near
my skin—or anywhere else. I love the look and feel of wool, and
I absorbed very early the idea that knitting with wool was nobler
and classier than knitting with anything synthetic. This was in
New Jersey, in the 1970s, when I was in high school, and learning
to knit was a gesture in the direction of a vaguely sixties sense of
craft and authenticity. Wool was natural. Wool was Whole Earth
Catalog. Wool felt good on my fingers—even the slight edge of
itch was a tactile pleasure. I liked working with it. I was happy
to pay more for the thick skeins of 100% wool, and I disdained
the cheaper synthetics of the time—which, at least in my memory, were available in crass unnatural colors, and were strangely
puffy and alien to the touch. And those cut-price yarns were

clearly associated with the fabrics disdained by right-thinking hippie-leaning adolescents because they belonged so definitively to style-challenged leisure-suit-wearing grownups: Doubleknit. Polyester. Synthetics.

But even then, I couldn't comfortably wear wool anywhere near my skin. My drawers all through college, graduate school, medical school, held a succession of wool sweaters, not that I had knit for myself (I was more of an intermittent scarf knitter), but that I had at least bought with pride. When I was nineteen, in England with my parents, my father happily chose himself a Harris Tweed jacket, and I chose a lovely lavender crewneck shetland sweater, proud, like him, to be spending money on the real thing—but I never wore it. There was a beautiful gray Fair Isle sweater—was it a pullover or a cardigan? I can close my eyes and see the white and blue and gray Fair Isle pattern—never wore it. There were some glorious woolen shawls I bought in India as a medical student, when it turned out that January, the cold season, brought out the New Delhi shawl sellers, and I admired the graceful women keeping warm in embroidered wraps over their saris—two of those shawls are hanging in my closet now, but when I want a shawl, I reach for something made of silk or cotton or rayon.

So I like the feeling of woolen yarn running through my fingers, but I get itchy if woolen fabric is anywhere near my skin—even a couple of layers out. So much for the Whole Earth Catalog. And as I say, even as a teenager, I also tended to feel warmer than the people around me. And after I had children, my metabolism changed, and I found myself generally too warm for sweaters of any kind. To this day, year round, I wear my business jackets over sleeveless cotton garments; two real layers leave me too warm.

Why am I telling you this? It's my long-way-round lead-in

to mourning my mother, who as she got older was often cold, who liked her apartment overheated the way they overheat New York City apartments in buildings with lots of elderly people, my mother, who wore a winter coat on days that I went to meet her wearing a T-shirt—my mother, who let me knit for her. So it's my lead-in to describing the doleful, prolonged, and heartbreaking task of emptying her apartment, since she died last spring, and reclaiming the things that I knit for her.

I'm not going to catalog the categories of sorting my mother's stuff (books and more books, clothes, jewelry, manuscripts, endless unidentifiable travel souvenirs, photos, unmentionable boxes still packed from her previous move) or anatomize the sibling discussions about who does what or who gets what. Taking apart the apartment feels like taking apart a life, because that's what it is— or at least, like taking apart the carefully constructed exoskeleton, laid down over the years and the decades. The truth is, it's a very sadly recent apartment—sadly recent because my mother had, with great effort, on her part and on my part and on my brother's, moved out of the apartment where she and my father had lived for more than twenty years into a smaller, nicer apartment, right around the corner from me. And to get her moved, we had sorted through vast quantities of stuff, we had made all kinds of decisions—and then, as probably happens with every move, we had gotten tired of making all those decisions, and let the movers pack up a bunch of stuff we couldn't face sorting, or couldn't quite classify—so those unmentionable unopened boxes are waiting in the closet. But I had helped her unpack the clothes she wanted into her new drawers, alphabetize the books she had kept onto the shelves, hang the paintings, put the dishes in the kitchen cabinets, back in late 2012. And now, less than two years later, she was gone and lost and had taken with her all the meaning of those drawers and shelves and walls and bookcases. And her clothing became the garments left behind when the body has departed.

So when I started by blathering on about wool and how I can't wear wool and how I'm always warm, what I really wanted to say was this: my mother is gone. Her body is gone, a body I had come to know so well in so many ways—feeling her pressed close to me, holding my arm for guidance and safety as we moved about the city, supervising her medications and accompanying her to her doctors and her eye doctors as she tried to fend off the encroaching blindness that terrified her so—and then, in the terrible last two months, when she was sick, hospitalized, in pain and in terror and in confusion, the body that betrayed her and broke down. Her body is gone, and when I think about that, I start crying.

And among the clothing left in her apartment, in her closets and her drawers, now that her body is gone, are the pieces I knit for her, for my mother, who would let me work with wool. The vests were hung carefully in the dress-clothes closet, each in a plastic dry-cleaner bag. The ornamental scarves were in a bottom drawer. The outside clothing—the warm scarves and hats—were up on the shelf in the coat closet, with the gloves, above the winter coats she wore when the temperature dipped below sixty or so. The only major thing I couldn't find was a silver-gray sweater that I made her more than a decade ago out of bulky Icelandic wool, thick and rich and hairy stuff that I couldn't have worn on the coldest day of winter. It worked up fast, and it came out a little too large—but it was warm and heavy and I can picture her wearing it, but only in her old apartment. I can't find it now, and I can't remember seeing it in the new place, so I'm left wondering whether we lost it in transition somehow—or whether it's actually in one of the unmentionable boxes. I don't particularly want that sweater—obviously, even if it fit me, I wouldn't wear it. But I can't help looking at the brighter colors of the items that I have in front of me, and thinking of the gray sweater, which once kept her warm in her overheated old apartment, and of how much is lost and gone.

2. MAGIC AND MEMORY: *the two variegated woolen vests*

She wore these vests a lot. What should I do with them? There are a couple of vests, knitted in expensive hand-dyed variegated wool, wool I bought when her eyesight was better, and she could appreciate the mixtures of pink and mauve and blue and green and brown. She wore those vests a lot. The first one buttoned up the front, closed with a row of pricy ceramic buttons, little crafty jewels— but she told me that with her worsening eyesight, she couldn't manage the unbuttoning easily, so she kept it permanently buttoned, and took it off over her head. So the next one looked like a cardigan, with a fake seam up the front, but it didn't really open at all. She wore those vests a lot, and when I tell you that, of course, I'm trying to tell you that I took care of her, I did, I decorated her and kept her warm and made sure that everyone with any sense of fibers, fiber arts, or fashion would have known immediately to look at her, my mother was someone who mattered, someone for whom garments were knitted, in careful patterned stitches, out of expensive hand-dyed wool.

I want to make it clear that left to herself, my mother would have been perfectly fine wearing sweatshirts or a cast-off red cardigan sweater of mine that dates back to high school and is rather mysteriously constructed of fake leather patches and zip pockets and thick scratchy always-pilling maroon wool. I know I had that item with me in college—I thought it was rather cool, though I had moments of doubt about those zippers—but I didn't wear it much, because—well, you know about me. But somehow it ended up in my mother's closet, zippers gleaming, fake leather patches resplendent, wool pilling. She would have been happy to wear that sweater over her shirts and under her winter coat. But instead I made her the vests, and she wore them and wore them.

The first one, the pink and mauve one with the fancy ceramic buttons, is made of wool that we bought together (though I didn't tell her the price, which would have shocked her) and is knit in a pattern of triplets, knit 3 purl 3 (and then in the next row, I think, knitting the purl stitches and purling the knit stitches, so you end up with a kind of extended moss stitch). Whatever the exact details, it was a stitch pattern I was able to memorize, back when I was knitting the vest, a decade ago, and I can remember the kind of almost subconscious chant that played in my mind as I was knitting one two three purling one two three, and meantime doing whatever else I needed to do. I knit that vest through a lot of meetings, one two three, one two three. I knit it through Game 7 of the 2004 American League Championship Series, when the Red Sox triumphantly crushed the Yankees, in Yankee Stadium no less, and went on to the World Series, where they would win for the first time since 1918.

The second vest, thicker and brighter in reds and blues and purples, was made a year or two later in a kind of triumph; I could see that she was getting lots of use out of the first one, and thus I felt I had an excuse to buy another big bag of expensive wool. Another simple pattern of knit and purl, something I could memorize and carry with me, and the kind of pattern—and the kind of variegated wool—which doesn't really show the occasional mistake. But I look at that vest now and it's a little bit shadowed; it's wool I chose without consulting her, since looking at different choices would have been too harsh a reminder of her failing eyes, it's the one without buttons—since it was too hard to find the buttonholes.

My mother, as you can probably tell, was not much for fashion. She shopped—when she shopped at all—for cheapness and for what would give her no trouble. Anything which required special care—hand wash, hang dry, or, god forbid, dry clean—she regarded as not just problematic but as actually evil, morally dubious, or, at the very least, too fancy for the likes of her—by which she meant, morally dubious. She could carry off dramatic clothes; she actually aged into a rather distinguished septuagenarian, with a gleaming cap of short white hair (I probably don't have to tell you that she did not go to beauty parlors—when her eyes got too bad for her to cut her own hair with her nail scissors, she began going to places called Quick Cuts, or maybe Cheap Cuts, and then, when she could see even less, and she was more generally frightened about moving around the city, she let me take her to a place I found down in Greenwich Village where a kind lady tended to her eyebrows and her face, and a pleasant gentleman gave her speedy flattering haircuts—I didn't tell her how much they cost). My mother could carry off a scarlet silk Chinese jacket, or a plum velvet overshirt. But she used to tell me, almost accusingly, that when she wore the things that I gave her—or that I bought with her—or, as she might put it, that I made her buy—other people were always telling her how nice she looked. She made it clear that she was a little wary of me; I was somehow privy to the suspect secret signals which told other people what was plain (and cheap) and what was fancy. And of course, if you complimented her silk jacket or her velvet overshirt, she would respond, half proudly, half defensively, "My daughter bought it for me," or maybe, "My daughter chose it," in tones which made it clear that, left to herself, she would never have gone in for anything of the kind (if someone happened to compliment a garment she had chosen for herself, which, for obvious reasons, didn't happen so often, she would generally respond either by pointing out that she had bought it for almost nothing at a discount place, or by explaining that it came from a catalog of superwashable-guaranteed-to-last-forever travel garments, and could therefore be squished into a tiny little ball and packed into a baggie).

But she wore those two vests a lot, and she didn't mind being complimented on them. She professed herself surprised that everyone could tell right away that they were handmade, that people fingered the fancy yarn and played with the ornate buttons—but I think, dare I say it, that she was proud of them. Proud of the yarn, proud of the buttons, proud that the vests had been hand knitted for her. And I wrap her in those vests in my memory; when I try to remember her well, not sick, when I try to remember her happy in her world, I picture her in one of those vests—usually the one with the fancy buttons, knitted for her out of wool that we chose together.

3. THE USEFUL AND THE USELESS: *the hat and scarves*

So as I said, I knit a lot of scarves. They work well for the kind of take-it-along knitting that I do, pulling things out in meetings or on airplanes while I'm watching bad movies (I know that if I were a good person, I would be knitting bigger, more ambitious projects, even if they had to be made in pieces, but I'm really bad at putting things together—and yes, I suspect that's more than a metaphor. But I have quite a few unfinished projects lying around the place: an elaborate intarsia cardigan where I never made it through the second front, another simpler jacket that I think is actually complete, but I've misplaced the second sleeve, and another where I bogged down when I tried to figure out how the sleeves fit into the armholes). So the sweater and the vests for my mother were major projects—but there were a lot of smaller ones along the way. I emptied out the top of the coat closet in her apartment and found a pile of the things that she would put on as she was going out, in her constant effort to keep warm in the world.

There's a red hat I knit in some long ago phase of hat-knitting, red and pink, made of a slightly tweedy yarn—it's flat as a pie on top, a disk that swirls into a central bobble, and then textured on the sides, with bands of stockinette and reverse stockinette pouching out, and a rolled I-cord at the bottom. It's actually very big and stretchy—so big and stretchy that I stuffed all the scarves into it and carried it home as a kind of woolen bag full of small knitted items, to be laid out and reviewed, as if I were getting the exhibits ready for a glass case, the small items in the Museum of My Mother.

Here's a scarf I knit my mother that really worked for her—it's made out of a bulky wool, variegated again, blue and mauve, and I made it in a knit one purl one rib so it doesn't curl at the edges. I barely even remember knitting this—just the sense of satisfaction at how quickly it grew on the needles. She wore this one with her blue fleece coat which is the coat she wore when she thought it was cold but not freezing. When she thought it might be freezing, she had a down coat, and also an old heavy parka that had been my father's, but she saved those for really severe weather—the kind of weather when other people also wore winter coats. Most days, she wore that blue fleece jacket, and that's how I picture her, moving around the city, these last years. Days that we were going some-where together—to the doctor, the eye doctor, to the movies, to the place where they cut her hair—I would call her up and say, I'm coming to pick you up, I'll meet you on the corner (I could have said, wait for me in the lobby of your building, where you can sit, but I knew she wouldn't do that). And I would come down the street and see her waiting on the corner, in that blue fleece jacket, leaning forward a little in my direction, peering ahead, trying to recognize me as I came into view.

And here's a scarf that my younger son made for her—garter stitch in thick stripes of white, blue, black, gray, maroon. Back and forth, back and forth. It came out nice and thick and soft, and she wore this one as well. She expressed awe that he was able to knit—she had often expressed awe that I was able to knit, since she said she couldn't knit or crochet or sew. Or sometimes she said she had once knit something, long ago, but it had been a disaster. But my mother was a person curiously devoid of hobbies—there was something stripped-down about her. She had a list of interests, of things that she cared about, and it was a good list, even a great list (reading, writing, teaching, family, food, theater, New York City . . .) but she didn't have room for a whole lot of extra little interests around the edges. She thought it was peculiar that I knit, and after I took her shopping for yarn, I suspect she came to think of it as yet another way that I had found to spend money on unnecessary luxuries. But when her grandchild took up the needles, of course, it became yet another piece of evidence that he was unusually dexterous and intellectually gifted (actually, the scarf was the single knitting project that he ever finished).

So the two scarves from the coat closet were well used. But here's one from her bottom drawer that I don't think she wore very often, a silly ornamental number that I made out of a novelty yarn, pink and light blue with lots of big white bobbles. It's a thin scarf, meant to be slung around the neck as a dashing decoration. I went through a period of novelty yarn scarves at one point, grabbing up balls of ribbon yarn and eyelash yarn and bouclé yarn and yarn with slubs and bobbles. I gave many such scarves away as gifts, and I kept a few for myself, and to be honest, I very rarely wear them. And I can't look at my mother's scarf without remembering a conversation we had after I gave it to her—she had opened the present, admired the scarf, looped it around her neck. It's very nice, she said. It looks great, I said. I just bought some more yarn, I added, I'm going to get to work and make you another. My mother looked troubled. "But Perri," she said, "I only have one neck."

4. UNNECESSARY LUXURY: *the red shawl*

For my mother's eightieth birthday, six years ago, I decided to knit her a shawl. I had found a pattern I really liked, with two ribbed arms that you tied in front that opened up into a large shawl panel in the back, with alternating thick bands of stockinette and reverse stockinette—imagine wearing a cardigan sweater by tying the arms together around your neck, so that the sweater settles over your shoulders and back. That's what this was like, a big soft cloud over your back, and then these two ribbed handles that you could tie. The yarn I bought was the yarn for which the pattern was designed, luxury stuff, a silk and mohair blend in red and purple, with some silver metallic elements, shining against the scarlet. I can throw it over my shoulders now and feel it settle softly, and I can note the somewhat clumsy join on each side where I picked up and knit, probably with smaller needles, to make that glossy ribbed arm.

My mother, of course, wouldn't have noticed the clumsy join. And I can remember her unwrapping the shawl, on her eightieth birthday, in the course of a rather over-elaborate evening celebration that my brother and I had concocted, which included stops at his home and then at two different restaurants, and any number of toasts and speeches. She admired the shawl, of course, and I demonstrated the way she was supposed to tie the arms, and showed her how gracefully it would fall across her shoulders, and how it would keep her warm. She assured me that the colors were beautiful, as indeed they were—and still are.

I meant it as beauty and warmth, but I also meant it as luxury. I knew my mother wouldn't have been able to identify the yarn—she would probably have expressed surprise that yarn could be made of silk in the first place—and of course, I wasn't going to tell her how much it had cost, but I liked the idea of yarn so lavish and colors so opulent. I liked the idea of my mother wrapped in mohair-soft silken jewel tones. I liked the idea of keeping her warm in ways that went way beyond the practical.

It was warm and soft, all right, but I don't think she wore this much. Maybe she used it now and then as a scarf, just wrapped round her neck for warmth, but it wasn't really a convenient shape for that, and I didn't find it in the coat closet with her keep-you-warm-outside things, I found it in the bottom drawer with that frivolous novelty yarn scarf, and a bunch of other nice shawls which I never saw her wear, including one I had bought with her on our trip to India a decade ago. I'm not sure any of these were really even on her mental inventory of her garments—that is, of the ones she actually reached for. I think the truth is, my mother hated the idea of shawls. She wasn't ashamed of her age, and heaven knows she was often cold, but somehow, I think, shawl to her meant old lady, in a very particular and distasteful sense, and she wasn't going to give way.

And my mother was suspicious of luxury. On that trip to India, she told me over and over that she didn't need fancy hotels, she didn't need first-class train tickets. The two of us played a game, in fact, in which it was agreed between us that I was using her age as an excuse to travel in luxury, when in fact it was I, with my upscale tastes and my weak-minded love of creature comforts, who really needed the five-star accommodations, the air-conditioned train carriages, the taxis and hired cars. And for all I know it may have been true; my mother was tougher than I will ever be, in body, in mind, and in spirit. I was happy to smooth her way, and happy to let it be understood that in accepting a little coddling, she was actually indulging me.

So I'll try to wear this shawl every now and then, even though it's wool, even though I'm never cold. But I'll wear it in full awareness that my mother didn't, and I'll try to let it represent her refusal to compromise. She didn't mind being in her eighties, but she didn't want certain trappings which would render her, in her own mind, an old lady. It was a gesture of love on her part to accept a little luxury, but she never fully let down her guard.

THE COLLECTION

So obviously, I take the vests and the scarves and the shawl. I've already brought them back around the corner to my apartment, the vests on their hangers, swathed in their plastic dry cleaner bags, the shawl and scarves stuffed into that accommodating hat. And I'm making resolutions—I'll try to wear the shawl, the yarn is beautiful—it's wool, but I could put it over a thick shirt. But if I put it over a thick shirt, I'll feel much too warm. Or maybe I'll put it away and maybe one day I'll be an old lady and I'll be cold and I'll put it around my shoulders, and think about how my mother resisted. And the vests? I guess I fold them away somewhere. Maybe someday I'll be the right size—significantly thinner than I am now—and I'll put on the one with the fancy buttons and look at myself in the mirror and see my mother looking out.

I yearn for that glass case, for space to display and explain and exhibit and commemorate. The Museum of My Mother, hand-knitting collection. I would like to type out cards explaining the provenance of each item, to curate the yarn and the patterns and verify the dating. It would be one more way of holding on to the body that is no longer here, and the meaning of her life, of trying to hold on to the space in the world which for me will always belong to my mother. As we take apart her apartment, as we sort her possessions into categories, this particular category, this overflowing armload of knitted bits and pieces, represents years of mother-daughter back-and-forth. There's a certain amount of egocentric showing off, of course—the museum of things I made for my mother. The museum of my attempts to keep my mother warm. The museum of stitches to hold her close.

But of course, this is a time of taking rooms apart. My mother is gone, and she doesn't get a museum—or at least not the kind with glass display cases (actually, my mother would have been vastly entertained by the idea of anyone contemplating putting any of her possessions on display—her garments, her jewelry, her pots and pans—since it was an article of belief with her that she owned—and wanted—nothing of any value or elegance or distinction). The right thing to do, surely, is to hold on to the things that I knitted and recognize them as the powerful talismans that they are, and use them to remember all that mother-daughter back-and-forth. The museum will be my very private collection, and the stitches and patterns will represent for me the complex negotiations of caretaking and luxury, the politics of giving and receiving, and the joy of knitting for someone I loved so much, and attempting to warm and adorn that indomitable and very distinct body and mind and spirit.

how we spend our days

CHRISTINA BAKER KLINE

*Knitting her way through chemo and radiation would have
been helpful. So why couldn't the author do it?*

TWO YEARS AGO, WHEN I WAS IN THE MIDST OF TREAT-
ment for breast cancer, Susan, a dear friend, showed up
on my doorstep with a bag of yarn and two wooden needles. "I am going to teach you to knit," she announced. "This is
what got me through my own horrible year of treatment."

I admired the skein of yarn, its intricate pattern of moss and
teal and eggplant. I could see that it would yield a stunning scarf
or hat, one I would be proud to wear on my still-bald head. I listened while Susan enumerated the many pleasures of knitting—its
restorative nature, the way it tamps down anxiety and frees your
mind for contemplation.

And then I put her off. "Another day," I said. "I'm just a little
tired"—shamelessly using chemo as an excuse.

Susan did not take no for an answer. Through emails, phone
calls and the occasional drop-in visit over the next few weeks,
she gently pressed me: "Come on, let's get started. Ten minutes.
That's all it'll take to get you going." But I could not bring myself
to open that bag of yarn.

Susan didn't know that there was a time in my twenties when I knew how to knit and actually made several entire wool sweaters. When I was an impoverished graduate student, I needed a birthday gift for David, then my fiancé, now my husband. My mother, an avid knitter, not only bought the needles and yarn (a lovely heather gray, as I recall); she also guided me every step of the way. David wore his cable-knit sweater so often that the elbows frayed. After that I knitted several more sweaters, cerulean for myself, rose for my sister. And then I put the needles down and never picked them up again.

I hadn't wondered why I no longer knitted until Susan forced the issue. It was then I started thinking of my mother.

My mother was one of the most dynamic and brilliant women I have ever known. She was also mercurial and unfocused. This is a woman who, while raising four daughters, taught English literature at a community college, got her PhD in women's studies and became a state legislator. She lived in a constant state of interrogation: of herself, the people around her and the wider world.

She moved from one passion to the next like a tornado moving across a flat landscape, sweeping up everything in its path and flinging it aside—astrology, feminist activism, organic gardening. Knitting was no different. For a few years, skeins of yarn piled up in baskets around the house. There weren't enough humans in my mother's orbit to wear all the scarves and sweaters and hats she knitted. And then, as suddenly as she started, she lost interest, leaving needles still entwined in half-finished fragments.

This was around the same time that my mother's PhD dissertation, a biography of a white female Southern labor organizer, was published by a renowned university press. The glowing reviews brought her a contract to write a book about a New York feminist intellectual who was at the forefront of many important political struggles of the twentieth century. My mother signed the contract. And then she made choices at every opportunity that led her further away from the book. She got involved in local political skirmishes and distracting personal disputes, and spent hours preparing and cleaning up after dinner parties. She agreed to put her home on the local "historic homes" tour. She dug up and replanted dahlias. She rearranged the living room furniture and dumped out drawers, trying, with limited luck, to sort them.

As each year bled into the next, my mother resolved to find the time to write the book—time that inevitably evaporated for one reason or another. The editor was growing impatient. Dozens of yet-to-be-transcribed cassette tapes from my mother's interviews spilled out of boxes in her study. It weighed on her heavily. And still she didn't—couldn't—finish. Was she intimidated by the material? Ambivalent about her relationship to the subject? Overwhelmed by all the data? Undoubtedly; she said so many times. But doesn't every writer face these roadblocks? Why was it so impossible for her to finish?

The subject of my mother's still-unwritten biography died in 2007, at the age of ninety-seven. My mother died six years later, after a sudden and unexpected stroke at the age of seventy-three, just as I was beginning radiation therapy, eight months after starting cancer treatment. Those cassette tapes are still in her study, along with her manila files arranged by subject, reference books taking up half a dozen shelves.

ANNIE DILLARD ONCE wrote, "How we spend our days is, of course, how we spend our lives." This line has been a touchstone and a rallying cry for me as I've struggled to find time to write fiction while raising three boys, teaching, and working as a freelance editor. Ms. Dillard's words remind me that it is easy to let days go by without writing, but in doing so I am making a statement about what I value, what matters most to me.

When I start a new novel and find myself diverted by domestic activities, many of which I genuinely enjoy, I panic that I will never write another word. So, consciously and unconsciously, I have laid down certain rules for myself. I will not serve lunch to anyone in the middle of a workday. I rarely rearrange my furniture or cabinets; once I find a drawer for something, it stays there. I don't garden. And I don't knit.

Those stitches could be words. Knitting, for me, became a symbol of the oppressiveness of women's traditional roles as cooks, floor scrubbers and menders—ephemeral work that robbed them of time and energy and kept them tied to hearth and home, far from the wider (male) world of important insights and discoveries. My own work has felt so culled from the margins, so hard-won, that the idea of doing just about anything creative with my hands other than clutching a Pilot P-500 pen and scribbling words on a white college-ruled legal pad has felt like a betrayal.

This is absurd, of course. It's not as if there's a quantifiable amount of creative energy, and if I knit I will use it up. For many people—including Susan, who is a painter—the opposite is true. What her gentle prodding forced me to recognize is that my disdain for knitting hid a deeper truth: that I was afraid I would die, like my mother, with my own work unfinished.

I need to let my mother—and myself—off the hook. She lived the life she chose to live. Fully intellectually and emotionally engaged, she had streams of friends, and was married for fifty years to my devoted father. She left behind four daughters who benefited from her devotion to art and culture. She planted, she sewed, she simmered, she knitted. I have to believe that if she had genuinely wanted to finish the book, she would have.

Susan's yarn and homemade needles look pretty in a bowl on a shelf in my study. But they have come to feel like a rebuke. In honor of my mother, I am going to take those needles out of the bag and give Susan a call. These words are meant to be an essay. That yarn is meant to be a hat.

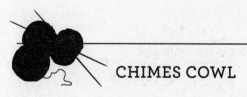

Loop
1914 South Street
Philadelphia, PA 19146
(215) 893-9939
www.loopyarn.com

CHIMES COWL

SIZE
One size, 5½ inches tall, 55 inches in circumference.

YARN
Loop Studio (100% superwash merino wool; 100g/350 yds): 1 skein MC, 1 skein CC; shown in Skylight and Smock

NEEDLES
40-inch size US6 circular needle

NOTIONS
stitch marker, darning needle

NOTES
Slip all stitches with yarn in back.

PATTERN
With CC over thumb and MC over index finger, CO 330sts using Long Tail Cast On. Place marker and join in the round being careful not to twist. Cut CC.

Continue with MC, *purl one round, knit one round; repeat from * once more.

Round 1: With MC, purl.

Round 2: With CC, *sl1, k1; rep from * to end.

Round 3: With CC, *sl1, p1; rep from * to end.

Round 4: With MC, knit.

Round 5: With MC, purl.

Round 6: With CC, *k1, sl1; rep from * to end.

Round 7: With CC, *p1, sl1; rep from * to end.

Round 8: With MC, knit.

Rep Rounds 1–8 until work measures approximately 5¼ inches, ending with round 8. Cut CC. Continue with MC, *purl one round, knit one round; rep from * once more. BO in purl.

Weave in ends and block lightly if needed.

on knitting

ANN LEARY

*The author can't tolerate knitters. Did the knitter who got
her through her difficult pregnancy and long hospitalization
in London ruin it for every other knitter to come?*

THEY'RE BANNED FROM AIR-TRAVEL NOW, THANK
God, but you still see them on trains, buses, park
benches and in coffee shops. They can be found in great
abundance in 12-step meetings and other group therapy settings,
and if you're not careful about whom you invite into your home,
you might find one in your own living room. Yes, I'm talking
about knitters.

I don't like knitters. I have nothing against people who knit
in private. It's really of no concern to me what people choose to
do in the privacy of their own homes. And certainly, I have nothing against professional knitters; the world must be scarved. No,
I mean the public knitters, the ones who want to shove it in your
face all the time.

Full reveal: I am unable to knit. I lack the dexterity. I have the
fine motor skills of a four-year-old. So I admit that it might be envy
that fuels my hate, but there's something else, and I know I'm not
alone. If the public knitter thought her behavior was pleasing to

others, she wouldn't be so stealthy about it. She'd carry her handi-work and her tools around in the open. Instead, the knitter will wander into a room like any other person, carrying a normal-look-ing bag, usually a tote. If the tote is quilted or felted, or in any other way appears to be handmade, you're right to be suspicious. Don't rush to judgment solely based on this accessory. A dear aunt or a mother might have made the bag. In private. It could contain anything—magazines, books or a snack. But keep in mind, this is how she works, the knitter. This is how she insinuates herself into polite society. When she sits down, this is the time to assess her carefully. Look for this tell: she will almost always take a moment, just after she settles herself into her chair, to smile thoughtfully at the air in front of her. If you are able to do so, leave now. Often, this is not possible and you will be forced to watch as she reaches into that seemingly benign satchel and extracts her instruments of torture—her yarn and needles and whatever she is currently knit-ting. Try as you might, you will be unable to avoid glancing at her handiwork, and when you do, you will catch the knitter's satisfied little nod as she flattens the woven panel out on her lap and counts the stitches. The little nod is meant for you and everybody else in the room. "Yes," the little nod says, "I thought so. I am perfect."

Does my hatred seem petty and unwarranted? Here's another reveal: I fell in love with a knitter once, and perhaps herein lies the root of my intolerance. Perhaps I hold all knitters up to too high a standard. I compare them to her, and they will always fall short. It happened when I was confined to a hospital bed in Lon-don. She and I were both young. Yes, my knitter was female and I am heterosexual, but I was in a maternity ward in a foreign city, surrounded by women. Things happen in institutions.

I was in the ward because my husband and I had the opportu-nity to go to London for a weekend. He had been hired by the BBC to appear on a late-night comedy show. I was six months pregnant. The day after we arrived, I went into preterm labor and though we had packed for two nights, it would be six months before we would return to the United States with our son Jack.

So, it was a difficult time.

I was admitted to University College Hospital in London. We learned later that we were quite lucky that Jack was born in this particular National Health Service hospital as it has one of the best neonatal units in the world. But at the time, I was too busy crying and fretting and torturing myself for choosing to accompany Denis on the trip. I was told I must remain on bedrest, there at that hospital, until the baby was born. They would try to prevent the onset of labor for as long as possible.

It was 1990. We didn't have cell phones. We didn't have laptops. There were no TVs in the maternity ward; it would have been annoying if there had been, given that there were eight of us in one large room. But my point is, there was nothing to distract me from my obsessive rumination, the persistent why, why, why?

Why me? Why us? Why did I get on the plane? Why did I carry my suitcase?

I tried to read, but couldn't focus on more than one word at a time. I flipped through magazines, stared at pictures. *Why? Why? Why?* Also, I couldn't stop crying, which was annoying to the other patients and medical staff.

Finally, one of the nurses, a very pretty, soft-spoken Irish girl named Claire, informed me that she thought knitting might help me. I needed something to keep me busy. She thought knitting might relax me. She would teach me how. The next night, she actually brought me knitting needles and yarn and in between chart notations and blood pressure readings, she sat beside my bed and showed me how to knit.

"First, you tie a knot, just like this," she said, and fastened a little knot on one of the long plastic knitting needles. "Then you have to cast on the first row." She held her thumb and index finger up and showed me how to take the needle and push it up with the thumb, over the tip of the needle, and then down to rest along the index finger.

"Oh, wouldn't it be lovely to have a jumper that you knit yourself for your little one?' she asked, repeating the loop, finger, thumb procedure. She crisscrossed the tips of the needles, back and forth, back and forth, until she had a row of tidy loops lined up on one of the needles.

"I'll be right back, now you hold this," she said, scurrying off to attend to a patient, and I sat with the needles in my hands, blinking at the tiny row of loops. When she returned, I carefully handed the needles and yarn back to her and she began, effortlessly, to knit.

Since that time, I have indulged in many things that are considered therapeutic. I've cuddled babies, watched the birth of a foal. I've meditated, bathed in spas, had "healing" massages, but nothing has ever soothed me quite the way that watching Nurse Claire knitting soothed me that day in that strange, lonely ward. She spoke as she knit, describing her home in Belfast and her flat in Maida Vale. The language she spoke was English, but the way she pronounced the words was Irish, they were pretty words, spoken quietly, with a sweet breathiness that accompanied the consonants. The way she pronounced the word knitting, not "nidding" as we Americans say, but "knitting." With that sweet breathiness. Her fingers were so delicate.

The gentle stabbing of the needles, the clear clacking sound as they met, and the graceful arching patterns performed by Claire's hands had me almost instantly lulled into a sort of trance. She knit a few rows and talked to me about her mother who had taught her to knit as a little girl, her roommate who was French, her dislike of all fish except for salmon, the weather, the Royals. I wasn't crying anymore. I was melting into the music created by her voice and the tapping of the needles.

"There," she said, after knitting a few rows, "Now you have a go."

"Please," I begged, "don't stop. I don't really understand. I need to watch you knit a little more, then I'll get the hang of it."

So she clickety-clacked away, describing her flatmates and a party they had thrown the night before for a friend who was moving back to Ireland. I looked around me. Though I had been in the ward for days, I was suddenly seeing it for the first time. Visiting hours were over; the boyfriends and husbands had all gone home. We were all women now. In the bed next to me, a nurse was strapping a fetal heart monitor around a pregnant belly and then the room was filled with the *swoosh, swoosh, swoosh* of a baby's heart beating, many fathoms deep. I touched my belly and my own small baby rolled leisurely against my hand.

"Your turn," Claire said, trying, once again, to hand the knitting off to me.

"Just let me watch a little more. I think I'm starting to understand it. I just need to watch," I whispered. "Just a little more."

And she began a new row. *Tap, tap tap. Clickety, clickety, clickety, click.*

"It's only tricky at the start," she said, "Soon you'll be knitting away without so much as a glance at what you're doing."

As she came to the end of each row, I feared she would try to hand the whole thing back to me. I didn't want her to stop, so I asked her about her brothers and sisters. I asked about her boyfriends. My eyes never left her hands, they began moving faster, her little fingertips tamping the yarn, the needles sliding up, down, up, down. It wasn't that I forgot where I was. I didn't forget my predicament—that would have been impossible. Instead, I found myself in a place I had not fully understood until that moment. I felt I belonged there in that room, there with the soft conversations of women all around me, there, next to the gentle *swoosh, swoosh, swoosh* of an unborn heart. There, watching sweet Claire, knitting something warm.

the dinosaur sweater

CAROLINE LEAVITT

Her husband asked for a sweater with brontosauruses on it.
If she knit it for him, would their marriage be saved?

I SUPPOSE YOU COULD SAY THAT A KNITTING PROJECT ended my first marriage.

Back then, I knit almost all the time because my husband Tom was never home. A lawyer, he left at six in the morning and came home around midnight, and was almost always unreachable by phone. I was really young, barely grazing the beginning of my twenties, and maybe I was a little stupid, too, because I never thought to ask him why he came home so late, why he never called me and I could never call him.

We were living in Cleveland, his hometown, a city I came to hate almost immediately. I wanted the buzz and heat of New York City, where my friends were, but my husband's job was in a town that seemed like a stomach cramp to me. There wasn't much energy, and though there was some culture, people seemed to feel that if you weren't in your pajamas and in bed watching TV by eight at night, there was something wrong with you. Still, I made a few friends, I got a part-time job at an alternative high school, teaching kids who had been kicked out of their regular schools. I spent my mornings writing, and then during those long, lonely evenings, I knit. And as the evenings grew longer, I began to want to challenge myself, to lose myself in a project so intricate I might not notice that Tom still wasn't home and I was alone. I taught myself intarsia and then graduated to complicated tableaux I mapped out on graph paper, color-coding every stitch. The hours zoomed by and I was so very grateful.

I made baby sweaters with a line of elephants marching across the chest for my brand-new nephew. I knit a scarf with maple leaves and giraffes on it for my sister. I wasn't sure why, but I never made anything for myself, and I never made anything for Tom. He always shrugged off my offers to make him a sweater or even a vest, insisting he didn't wear them. "They itch," he said, even though I told him I'd make something in cashmere, I'd find the softest baby yarn. "Not for me," he said. I hid my hurt. I didn't tell him that part of why I wanted to make him something was that I loved the idea of him in a creamy white fisherman sweater, a seed-stitched pullover, a fine-gauged V-neck vest he could wear under his jacket when he was in court. It was a part of me he would be wearing, a reminder of how much he was loved, and who wouldn't want that? He'd be carrying me with him.

One evening, I was finishing up a baby blanket when Tom came home and admired it. "You know," he said, "I changed my mind. I do want a sweater from you."

"Really? You do?"

"I want a sweater with brontosauruses on it."

"I can do that."

"Really? Can you make one of them grazing on vegetation?"

"I can do that, too."

"Front and back?"

"Yup."

The thing was, I really had no idea if I could pull this off or not, but I was basking in his interest. Tom's sweater would be much more complicated than any of the other sweaters I'd designed. I spent months mapping the sweater out on graph paper, figuring out each color, each nuance until I had the scenario: two brontosauruses with lovely long necks, one stretched upward, one grazing on the green grasses below. I'd do another dinosaur on the back, and I'd do it all on a creamy beige background.

I spent hours in the yarn shop finding just the right colors, the delectable tan, three shades of green for the vegetation, and a deep rust red for accents. I even bought a little bit of black yarn so I could give the dinosaurs toenails and dark pupils for their eyes. I spent a fortune, but I didn't care because it was for Tom.

Every night he asked, "How's my sweater coming?" but I refused to tell him. I wanted him to see it when it was finished, when it was so glorious that he was going to be shocked. I wanted him to think: *This is my wife in every stitch. Look at what she can do. Look how lucky I am to have someone like her.*

I was halfway through the front when Tom began not to come home. I'd finally fall asleep and wake up in the morning to find his side of the bed empty. He did this once, twice, three times, and he always had the same excuse, and it always sounded at least sort of valid. "I was working so late I fell asleep at the office," he said. "I looked up and it was three in the morning, and how could I wake you?"

I believed him.

I made myself as busy as I could to stave off my loneliness. I was writing my second novel, in the tiny alcove we'd made into my studio. To fill up the hours, I took ballet, and evenings, I came home and knit, stopping only to make dinner for myself. The dinosaur sweater began to take on a life of its own, a personality. Tom and I didn't really socialize because he was so busy, but when we did go out to dinner with friends, they asked me about the sweater. "Tom keeps talking about it," they said, and I beamed, pleased, because if he was talking about the sweater, wasn't he thinking about me?

It took me four months to make that sweater, and when I finished I carefully blocked it. I stared at it in wonder. Every part of it was a story. The brontosaurus eating leaves was finished right before my birthday. The cloud in the sky was done in the spring. The dinosaur on the back, his mouth open, was finished on our anniversary. I laid the sweater out on the dining room table to surprise Tom, and when he came home and saw it, he was lit from within. "Oh my God," he said, and shucked off his jacket to pull it on. He admired himself in the mirror in our bedroom, smoothing it with his hands. "I never want to take it off," he told me.

He wore the sweater everywhere. To visit his parents, to go out to dinner. He told me that people stopped him in the street to ask about the sweater. Sometimes, when he wasn't wearing it, I spread it on the bed just to bask in it, the way the brontosaurus neck sloped into the grasses, that brilliant shock of red in the grass, so subtle, and yet it made everything seem to vibrate with life.

I hand-washed it. I didn't want it to unravel.

Ah yes, that was for my marriage to do.

Tom began going on business trips. "I'll call you when I know where I'm staying," he told me, and then he never did. I never thought to call his office to find out his hotel, and when he came home, he teased me out of my anger. "Come on," he said. "I forgot."

But it began happening more and more. Worse, when he was home, he now seemed sullen and furious. "Did I do something?" I asked him, and he just glowered. Weekends, he said he had to work. He had to work nights, too, and early mornings, and when

I asked him if we could take a vacation, he said his workload made that impossible.

I didn't know what to do. I felt like I was living alone, and for all purposes, I was, eating all my meals by myself or with friends, seeing him only for the briefest moments before he left for work, and when he came home he was always in that dark, swampy mood. We stopped having sex, and in bed, he curled his body to the farthest corner. I was too scared to talk about any of it with my friends, maybe because I was afraid of their answers.

One night, in bed, when I reached for him, he went rigid.

"I'm tired," he complained. "I just want to sleep."

"You have to tell me what's wrong," I begged. "Are we in trouble?"

He looked at me as if I was a stranger. We both sat up in bed.

"Should we get counseling?"

He hesitated and I thought, maybe this is what we would do. We would sit down together, we would figure it out. Marriages could be patched together. But his mouth hardened into a line. "I want a divorce," he said.

Stunned, I stared helplessly at him. Now, all those business trips, those late nights started to form a different scenario for me. "Oh my God, there's someone else," I said.

"No."

"Would you tell me if there was someone else?"

He was quiet for a moment. "No," he said, and I burst into tears because I knew what he was really saying. Yes. Of course there is. Yes. Yes. Yes.

HE MOVED IN with his parents, who lived ten minutes away. The funny thing was, I saw him more than when we were a couple, because he was always dropping by, even though I told him not to.

He had to get clothing. He wanted to check the mail. Once I came home to find him putting mothballs in the pockets of our winter coats. He looked at me as if nothing were wrong. "Get out," I shouted, and he did.

Taking apart a marriage was like taking apart a sweater. Some people did it carefully, so they could reuse the yarn and reknit it. Others made mistakes that could be repaired if you undid some of the knitting. But sometimes nothing could put things back together again. You just had to rip it all apart.

Mostly what I did was sob. I quit my job teaching. I walked into the ballet studio and told my teacher that I was leaving class, and when I started to cry she soothed, "Oh honey," and even though she barely knew me, she moved me into her apartment for a week, taking care of me, staying up until all hours with me watching old movies.

I finally went home, which no longer felt like home. I was in Cleveland only because of Tom, and I couldn't imagine staying here without him, running into him, hearing his name in the local news for some big case. So I made plans to stay with friends in Manhattan until I could find my own place. I called my agent who promptly gave me a part-time job helping out at the agency until I was on my feet.

I began packing my things. I went through our closet and every item of clothes reminded me of the day I wore it with him. And then I remembered, the dinosaur sweater, and I went to his dresser and took it out. It was soft and beautiful. But it represented something that was no longer true, a marriage that was no longer there, and I needed to face it. I went into the kitchen to get the scissors and came back and then I cut the sweater down the center. I stuffed it in the kitchen trash, on top of the tofu box and banana peels. It didn't belong to him anymore. Every emotion

THE DINOSAUR SWEATER · 175

I had knit into the sweater—love and need and devotion—was meaningless now.

The next day, when I came home from work, the sweater was damp, spread out to dry on a towel, the cut stitched together. Tom must have done this. The sweater was still beautiful, and even though Tom had done a clumsy job, it was still wearable. I went to the kitchen for the scissors and this time, cut the sweater into tinier pieces, until I was surrounded by minuscule swatches. There it was. Those months of work, the beautiful yarn, my marriage, the dinosaur. All of them extinct.

I left the pieces where they were and I booked a train to New York City.

Every time I had ever traveled, I had taken a knitting project with me. The clack of the needles soothed me. I loved the whole rhythm of the work. But this time, I left my needles, my yarns behind. I never wanted to knit again. All of that life was ripped out, just the way I would an errant seam, and I told myself I wouldn't miss it.

New York City was an explosion of colors and I fell in love with it the moment I saw a man walking by with a branch tied to his head. I was in Manhattan six months, living in a shoebox studio on 24th Street, with a slanted floor and an occasional mouse. I hadn't filed for divorce and neither had Tom, and every few weeks he called me, his voice sad. "Maybe we can work it out," he said, but the truth was, I wasn't quite sure I wanted to anymore.

One evening, I got a call, from a woman I'll call Stella, who said that she was Tom's girlfriend, that she had been Tom's girlfriend for five years and she wanted to know when I was going to divorce him. Horrified, I gripped the phone. I listened to her tell me about the trips they had taken together, the way she would slip into our home when I was at work. I was starving for knowledge, but at the same time, I listened as if all that had happened to a different person, a person who didn't now have lots of friends and go out every night to plays, and ballet and dinner. A person who wasn't happy. "Why didn't you clean the apartment more?" she said. "Why didn't you iron his shirts instead of sending them out? I had to do it for him. Don't you like a nice home?"

I looked around my studio, piled with books, the slanted floor, the chipped ceiling. I loved that tiny apartment more than I had ever loved our big, gracious home in Cleveland, and now, knowing what had really happened with Tom and me, I loved it even more.

"Are you angry with me?" Stella said.

I thought about it for a moment. "No. Grateful," I said. "Thanks for letting me know," I told her, and hung up. Then I began immediately looking for a divorce lawyer.

AS SOON AS I served Tom with divorce papers, I began missing the dinosaur sweater. I found myself dreaming about it. I remembered how glorious it was. When I told my friends about it, they shook their heads. "You should have taken that sweater for yourself," they told me, and they were right. I could have worn it in the Village and people would have stopped me and asked about it, or maybe they wouldn't have, but I would have just felt good wearing it. Proud. I could never re-create that sweater. I'd have to graph it out again, which had taken me weeks. I'd have to devote hours to it that I no longer had because my life was now so busy, so full, so happy.

One day, I was walking in the Village when I passed a yarn store and I stopped. My hands hadn't touched yarn since I left Tom. I hadn't craved the click of the needles. I walked inside and fingered the yarns, and just the feel of the yarn made me suddenly yearn to knit. I ended up buying a soft rosy wool for a scarf, a pattern so simple I could knit it while having conversations with friends or sitting in on a class. I began to knit on the subway, in Central Park, in the cafes, and the more I knit, the happier I felt. Knitting was different now. It was no longer a way to make less of what was going on in my life, a way to help me forget my pain. Instead, it was now a way to enhance what was good. It was a beautiful scarf, and maybe it wasn't as intricate or special as the dinosaur sweater, but in a way, it was even better.

the thirty-first stocking

LAURA LIPPMAN

*When the author agreed to give up Christmas and raise her
daughter Jewish, she thought it would be easy. But was it?*

WHEN MY MOTHER WAS TWENTY-ONE, MAYBE
twenty-two, she bought a knitting kit at an Atlanta
notions store. The kit had everything one needed to
make a personalized Christmas stocking—a pattern, red, green
and white yarn, jingle bells, a small cloud of angora for Santa
Claus's beard. Already a proficient knitter—argyle socks had been
the rage during her high school years—she needed less than a
week to make a stocking for her young cousin Peg.

Over the next five decades, she would make twenty-nine more
stockings. For herself, for her new husband, Theo. For their first
daughter, born in 1956. For the second daughter—me—born in
1959. A nephew, a niece. Family friends. My sister's husband. The
nephew's wife. My first husband, although not my second. The
kits were discontinued at some point, but my mother had kept
the instructions and the pattern. Even when there was that long
stocking-free stretch through the 1970s and into the '80s, she
saved those instructions. Her friends began having grandchildren
and the stockings started again.

Finally, in 2010, I could tell my mother that *she* was going to be a grandmother. Given that I was fifty, she had pretty much given up hope.

"Do you want me to make a stocking?" Of course I did.

But the thirty-first stocking turned out to be problematic from the start.

To begin with, there was the matter of the name. My husband and I had long agreed that, should we ever have a daughter, we would call her Georgia Rae. He told people we had chosen the name to honor Ray Charles and the song he had popularized, "Georgia on My Mind." I, ever more pedantic, explained we had appropriated the name from a singer-songwriter, John Hiatt. *He* had named his daughter for Ray Charles and then written a song about her; we were just copycats. But I liked the "Georgia" because it was a reference to the state where I was born, the state where most of my relatives still lived.

And what if it was a boy? I yearned to use some variation of my father's name, but my husband was adamant: No names for living people. That's Jewish law and he's a Jew, the kind of Jew who says things like: "The synagogue I fail to attend must be conservative." A Jew who eats bacon and shellfish and marries shiksas, but wants to raise his children as Jews. Upon our marriage, I readily agreed to that condition, although, unlike his previous wife, I didn't convert. I was a Protestant, the kind of Protestant who says things like: "I don't see the point of being non-observant in two religions."

But I did see the point of getting my own way, whenever possible. And I had covered politics quite a bit during my twenty-year newspaper career; I knew how consensus was made, how to build alliances. I waylaid my stepson, already a talented jazz pianist as a teenager, and brokered a deal: I would let him name his future baby brother Theolonious, as long as the boy was called Theo. He said he would throw his support behind me if the middle name were Parker, for another one of his jazz heroes. Done! We presented the name to his father, a fait accompli. Theolonious Parker Simon, Theo for short.

We planned to shorten the girl's name as well, calling her Rae. But when she showed up in May 2010, she was so clearly a girl meant to be called Georgia Rae. As the John Hiatt song begins: "I know a girl mess with your mind." Boy, did she. The force of her personality was evident before she was twenty-four hours old. She was born the night of a full moon, part of a bumper crop of babies. Twenty-two children were delivered in the hospital that night. We like to say that only nineteen went home with personalities, that Georgia Rae had crept from bed to bed, sucking the life force out of at least three.

But if Georgia Rae was big enough to handle her name, her stocking was not. At least, that is the story my mother tells now, making excuses for the truncated RAE at the top of the thirty-first stocking. Ever gallant, she claims that she chose to use only the second name because Georgia Rae didn't fit. I never point out that she made a stocking for her niece, Elizabeth, whose name is only one letter shorter, or that she has a stocking in her own name, Madeline. She is, as she is inclined to do, letting me off the hook. I was the one who told her to make the stocking for "Rae." It was the first time my daughter put me on notice that she would decide who she was, how she would be known.

Still, I looked forward to filling that misnamed stocking. In my childhood, stocking gifts were often the best thing about Christmas Day, the true surprises, things not found on any list. A painted box with a unicorn on its cover—that was from my mom. A brass monkey that functioned as a card holder. "I just thought it looked like something you would love," said my first husband, and he was right. Things like that. I knew our daughter, not quite seven months old on Christmas Day, would have little use for whatever came out of her stocking on that first Christmas, but one day—oh, wait, she was going to be raised a Jew. Well, her brother, who had been raised a Jew by a woman who had gone to the trouble of converting, had still enjoyed all the Christmas rituals. There was no reason that Georgia Rae could not.

But first she had to become a Jew, officially. The daughter of a non-Jewish woman is not a Jew, not until she's taken a *mikvah*, the ritual bath. Been dunked, in my husband's vernacular. To become a Jew, she would have to be completely immersed in a ritual bath as rabbis sang a blessing. And in order for our daughter to be dunked, we had to pass a test of sorts.

On a bitter cold day in early December, we drove to a synagogue in Washington, D.C., and sat before a panel of three rabbis, including the one who officiated at my stepson's bar mitzvah. There was bad blood between this rabbi and me, although she doesn't know it. She prohibited me from being on the *bima* during my stepson's bar mitzvah because I am not a Jew. Other non-Jews were up there that day, but she didn't realize that, so she didn't ban them. My husband wishes I would stop bringing this up. He points out that I could have participated during a part of the service when the Torah was not open. He believes the rabbi acted appropriately. I think she was trying to shake my husband down because he didn't have an official "get"—the document that Jewish husbands are obligated to present during a divorce. At any rate, I was still holding that grudge three years later.

But on this particular day, I was a supplicant. So I behaved very well, facing that panel of three rabbis. I explained that I had chosen not to convert, but I would do everything I could to help my husband raise our daughter as a Jew. ("Not in your synagogue," I thought of my rabbi-nemesis.) After all, I had done that for my stepson—driving him to Hebrew school and, well, driving him home from Hebrew school.

What about Christmas? one of the rabbis asked me.

Oh yeah. Christmas. What about it? I had not put up a Christmas tree or hung my stocking since my husband and I began living together eight years earlier. Christmas decorations really bugged him and I had discovered that I didn't miss them at all. No more pine needles to vacuum. We exchanged gifts on December 25 and then, in the great Jewish tradition, went to the movies and ate Chinese food. I had experience celebrating Christmas this way. As it happens, my first husband was born on Christmas Day and I had always tried to make the day about him, not the holiday. So we went to the movies and ate Chinese food. Christmas really wasn't that important to me. Besides, this wasn't a legally binding conversation. I could do whatever I wanted once I left that synagogue.

"We will not observe Christmas in our household," I told the rabbis in a sudden burst of inspiration. "I will pack up her stocking, the ornaments I own and take them to my sister's house. We will explain Christmas to her as a practice observed by others, but not us. I don't believe that people should cherry-pick religions for the best parts. You have to choose one and stick with it."

We passed the test and descended to the basement, where there was a small round pool, no different from any health club Jacuzzi to my eyes. My husband, in a bathing suit, took hold of our naked child and pulled her under the water in one quick swoosh, making sure not to miss a patch of skin. When they surfaced, she looked furious, on the verge of a vengeful scream. But then the rabbis began to sing and she was distracted by the Hebrew syllables bouncing off the tiles in the steamy air. It was beautiful.

On the drive home, I all but cackled at how slick I had been in front of the rabbis. I told the story over and over to the family that gathered that night to celebrate. *I was going to give up Christmas! I was going to take all the ornaments to my sister's house!* I was like the French knight in *Monty Python and the Holy Grail*, sniggering at King Arthur and his knights in their futile quest. "I tol' them we haven't got one!"

Lies have a strange way of making themselves true. Less than two weeks later, I packed up all the Christmas things in my household and took them to my sister's. The thirty-first stocking was not hung that year. Almost four years later, it has yet to be hung. We go to my sister's house on Christmas Eve, but the things I gave her remain boxed. Maybe this year, now that Georgia Rae is more aware, we will let her have a stocking over there. Last year, contemplating the Christmas season's riches, she moaned to me: "I wish I weren't Jewish." She asked for lights on the house, but my husband could not bear it, not even in Hanukkah-friendly blue and white. It turns out that he is also the kind of a Jew who would be ashamed—his word—if another Jew came to his home in December and saw lights. We compromised and began hanging lights during Mardi Gras season, in strings of purple, green and gold. We tell people that's our true religion, anyway. Secular humanist Mardi Gras-ism with a side of voodoo.

Meanwhile, I kept my promise to the rabbis, trying to help my husband raise our daughter as a Jew. I learned to make challah. I bought a Kiddush cup. I made latkes for Hanukkah. When my husband had to travel for work, I downloaded prayers from the Internet, threw a napkin on my head and, sneaking a peek through my eyelashes, recited the words phonetically. *Baruch atoy adonai . . .* Losing Christmas was easy.

I hadn't counted on losing God, too.

. . .

NOW IF YOU had asked me five years ago to define my religious beliefs, I would have leaned hard on the word, "Deist." I had been brought up as a Presbyterian, a word often used as a slur by my husband and in-laws, a way of connoting someone prissy or bland, someone who eats a bagel with butter on it. I have never eaten a bagel with butter on it. I went to church through the age of twelve, then stopped, a decision my parents supported. I came to believe there was a central intelligence to the universe, but accepted that it was so multidimensional that I could never understand it. This power did not, as I understood it, respond to petitionary prayer. But there was no harm in speaking to God, trying to sort things out. I had been talking to God all my life, since I was four or five. As a child, I imagined a man in a blue robe and a black crew cut, leaning over a cloud, his arms open as if to embrace me. I talked to God more often than anyone knew. I made promises, most of which I broke. Yet I believed in him.

Then, one day, I found I could no longer justify this belief. It didn't happen in a flash. But things started to unravel in front of the rabbis when I blithely said: "I don't believe in cherry-picking religions." Wasn't I cherry-picking? I didn't believe in hell. Heck, I didn't believe in any afterlife, much as I yearned to. I was skeptical of all organized faiths. I couldn't embrace any aspect of religion that seemed to exist only to reward belief. Yet—I had believed in God and now I didn't. It was hard. It's still hard. If someone asked me point-blank how I define myself, I would probably say that I'm an atheist who yearns to be proven wrong. Not because I want an afterlife. Not because I fear hell. I want there to be a God because I really miss talking to him.

In that way, God is not unlike my first husband, the Christmas

Day baby whose stocking also was put away, many years ago, and remains in an unmarked box somewhere in my basement. What number was that? The twenty-third or the twenty-fourth? It's easy to lose count. But that was the first stocking to be retired, strictly speaking. And everyone for whom my mother has made a stocking is still alive as far as I know. Meanwhile, my mother's friends are having great-grandchildren now. A thirty-second stocking seems possible, maybe a thirty-third.

But the stockings can't go on forever. Nothing does. One day, the stockings will end and I won't even have my crew-cut God for comfort. Still, I have kept my word to the rabbis, and there is honor in that. Atheists, who have no one to make rules for us, have to figure out right and wrong for ourselves. I tell my daughter that our household has one inviolate rule: Keep your promises, don't ever lie.

Luckily, the rabbis didn't think to ask me about Easter.

positive capability

MAILE MELOY

*Over time, the author changes her mind about how knitting
and writing are the same—and how they are different.*

M
Y MOTHER WAS TAUGHT TO KNIT AND CROCHET
and sew, as a girl of the fifties. When my brother and
I were babies, she made us matching Christmas stockings. They each have Santa's face on the front, with a fuzzy white
angora beard and a bell on his hat. Our names are on the cuffs,
and mine has my birthday, but by the time my brother was born,
our mother had other things on her mind, and Colin's birthday
has my year.

"It's an easy mistake," he says now, to tease her. "When you're
writing something down quickly. Like when you're *knitting* it, *row
by row.*"

"I always meant to fix it!" she says.

That she was distracted is understandable. She had two tiny
children, and I don't know how she could focus on anything.

Our parents, divorced, had joint custody, so we carried the
Santa stockings from one house to the other and got them filled
twice, but it never occurred to me to wonder how the stockings
were made, or to ask to be shown how to do it. I was a feminist

child of the eighties, and listened to *Free to Be You and Me* and read *Ms.* magazine. I was not taught to knit or crochet or sew. I took wood shop and metal shop in middle school, and made a serviceable spatula that's still in use.

I would never have learned to knit if my friend Beth hadn't brought, ten years ago, a wrapped starter knitting kit to one of those parties where you're supposed to open a present or steal one. I had the very first turn and opened her gift—a skein of confetti-colored yarn, wooden needles, a project bag, a promised lesson. No one stole it from me. They wanted less labor-intensive gifts. So Beth and I sat in a corner and she gave me the lesson, while the rest of the presents made the rounds.

The needles were like chubby pencils for preschoolers, and the yarn thick and variegated. I was clumsy, afraid of losing hold, and wrapped the yarn so tightly that the tip of my finger turned purple. Beth showed me a garter stitch, and I made a short, wide, unwearable scarf before I ran out of yarn. So I unraveled it and started over with a narrower scarf, but it was still too short to wrap around a neck. I understood that this had been a learning exercise, like practicing scales or writing stories that no one would see.

I bought some skinnier needles and many skeins of blue-gray yarn, and made a long scarf for my boyfriend. He still wears it now that he's my husband and it's kind of ratty. Once or twice a year he loses it and goes into a panic. I think it would be okay if it vanished, but it always turns up.

For my brother's first baby, I made a sweater that was essentially five potholders sewn together; the sleeves are potholders folded over. I tried making booties that were advertised as foolproof, but they came out like doll booties or tree ornaments, each one smaller than the last, so I never had a set. I had kept the rookie habit of knitting too tightly, and it drove real knitters crazy. Strangers would say, "Why are you doing that? Stop knitting so tightly. That's *not knitting!*"

I didn't understand what they meant. I had learned how to make the simplest stitches, but I had no comprehension. I didn't really know what a stitch was. I certainly couldn't find one if I dropped it.

Beth lived far away, so I found a knitting mentor close by. Whenever something baffling happened, I would take it to my friend Ann's door, up the street. She would squint at the project and say, "Oh, the stitch is right here, see? So just pull these rows out." She would tug and unravel them while I flinched and looked away. Then she would reach in for the dropped stitch and pull it up, cold-blooded as a surgeon.

"I'm trying to knit as tightly as you do, to match," she would say as she repaired the row. But it was impossible for her to match. It takes real determination and fear to knit that tightly. So there is always a scar to show where she operated: a raised row amid my freakishly tight weave.

MY BROTHER'S WIFE, Carson, is an extraordinary knitter, too, always with some cabled wonder under way, and I would never have foisted a sweater made of potholders on her firstborn if I had known how good she is. But since I'd outed myself as a limited knitter, I had nothing to prove. When she was pregnant a second time, I bought some stretchy, fuzzy yarn for a hat on circular needles, in interesting oranges and greens. A sophisticated yarn for a sophisticated baby.

I took it to Ann to check it out.

She said, "Wow, weird yarn. You'll have to make a gauge to see how it knits up." She tugged at it, feeling the way it stretched.

"I'm not making a gauge," I said.

She said, "I know, no one wants to make a gauge, but with this, you really have to."

I said, "I can't. I would rather make the hat, find it the wrong size, and start over, than make a gauge."

Ann shrugged cheerfully and said, "Okay."

I know it would be more efficient to make a gauge. I know my refusal means that I will never be a good knitter. I don't understand stitches, I don't know what the abbreviations mean in patterns, I'm impatient. And I have ambition only slightly above my skill level.

Ann guessed how many extra stitches to cast on to compensate for my crazy-tight knitting (I'd forgotten how to cast on), and helped me with the math for reducing the stitches at the top, and I went off to work. But something had happened since the last time I'd made a hat. Miraculously, my knitting had loosened up. I was no longer clinging to the yarn for dear life. And when I finished, the fuzzy hat was enormous. It would have fit a Halloween pumpkin, and it was splotchy and dark, the colors all fused together. I finished it on a trip with my grandmother, who has never liked to knit, and she was very kind about it. "He'll grow into it!" she said.

I used to think there was such a thing as negative-capability knitting, as in Keats's concept of negative capability: "that is when man is capable of being in uncertainties, mysteries, doubts, without any irritable reaching after fact and reason." Creative work is about process, and you shouldn't really know what you're doing when you're making something. It should be terrifying: that's when it's going well. The nature of stitches could remain a mystery!

But when I saw the mess I'd made of the baby hat, I started to revise my theory. Weird, unpredictable art isn't what you want for a newborn, and the hat was awful. I started over with some nice soft pale yarn, and made a hat of appropriate size and cuteness. And I started to think that what knitting really takes is *positive* capability: that is, understanding how stitches work, making a gauge without any irritable impatience, and having a plan.

MY HUSBAND'S SISTER-IN-LAW, Danie, is a librarian and sails as crew on a three-masted barkentine called the *Gazela*, built around 1901 from the timbers of an older ship (like the yarn from a recycled sweater), to fish the Grand Banks. Putting away sails in a locker last year, Danie hit her head and suffered post-concussive syndrome. Doctors advise concussion patients not to read or look at screens, which is tough for a librarian. Knitting is one of the few activities allowed.

So, with a librarian's capacity for meticulous attention, Danie began a double-knitted blanket, five feet by three feet, with the image of the *Gazela* and the name of the ship on both sides, to be sold to raise funds for the ship's preservation. First she had to create a pattern from photographs, which online pattern generators will do, but the ship's rigging is so intricate that Danie had to guess at which aspects of the photograph to include, and adjust once she saw the image rendered in stitches. And the blanket was so big that she had to make four patterns on graph paper, one for each quadrant, and fit them together. Where the patterns met, she had to improvise on the fly. And to get the letters to read the same on both sides of the blanket, she had to work out the double-knit pattern so that she was knitting two different letters, facing different ways, at the same time.

The yarn is fine-gauge, the letters perfect. Just describing the project makes my head hurt, and I don't have a concussion. (It might not have been the kind of knitting the doctors had in mind.) The finished blanket is a thing of beauty, and will raise a fortune for the Philadelphia Ship Preservation Guild. It's proof that positive capability works.

My mother has started knitting again, having abandoned it long ago. She's making a Christmas stocking for my husband, which moves him beyond words. He already gets a borrowed, ownerless stocking, filled with candies and wool socks and small flashlights and an orange in the toe. That a grown man might have his own designated homemade stocking, to be filled at two different houses each year, exceeds his expectations for adulthood. I tell him it's just because my parents don't like to wrap presents, but he knows better.

My mother was almost finished last Christmas, reducing the stocking's toe with a spiky cluster of double-pointed needles, when she left the project on a chair and my cousin sat on it. There was a howl of pain, and then a second howl when my mother saw all her loopy stitches waving free of their needles and slipping away. I don't know which of them got the worst of it, cousin or sock. My mother went to Carson to ask her to repair the damage, and watched anxiously while Carson studied the stitches and pulled some out, then dipped in with the needles to pluck the lost ones up. I am my mother's daughter, it turns out.

Knitting, I've come to think, is not about working in the dark and doing what you can, or doubt being your passion. Writing is about that. Knitting is about having a good light and a good friend to fix your mistakes. It's about setting aside time to think about the new baby, or the beloved wooden ship, or the man who will unstuff the stocking, while you work. It's tangible evidence of love, manifested through time, stitch by stitch. At least that's what it is for me, now, and all it needs to be.

knit your bit

STEWART O'NAN

*During World War I, the American Red Cross asked Americans
to send knitted goods to the soldiers overseas. The author
reminds us that we should knit for soldiers in every war.*

M Y GRANDFATHER WAS IN BALLOONS. THIS WAS IN
World War I, in France, in the winter of 1917. High
up, from a gondola tethered by a steel cable to a motorized winch below, he surveyed the snowy countryside, the fallow
fields stitched with trenches and pocked with craters, cranking a
boxy field telephone to call in the German troops' movements.
Only two men could fit in the gondola, which was unheated,
pushed by the winds and swallowed by low-hanging clouds, at the
mercy of enemy aces nicknamed balloon-busters. The winch was
slow, the engine unreliable in the cold. In case of aerial attack,
they were issued a new invention called a parachute. In training
outside of Omaha they'd witnessed a demonstration of the device
in which a man broke both his legs. Following the confused logic
of the skeptical, most refused to wear it.

Unhappily, the Marne shares the 49th parallel with Newfound-
land, and by December, more often than not they were grounded

by fog. They lived in mud, in canvas tents with only a central stove to keep them warm. Firewood was hard to find, and the most valuable commodity around camp wasn't whisky or cigarettes but dry socks. Like the doughboys, they lived in fear of trench foot and the surgeon's saw. They wrote their wives and sweethearts and mothers. All they wanted for Christmas was woolen socks.

They weren't alone. That first winter of the war, the U.S. Army was poorly prepared. The boots issued to soldiers weren't insulated and tended to split at the seams, the soles flopping loose. The men craftily began asking for boots two sizes too big so they could wear several pairs of socks underneath.

Realizing how great the need was, the American Red Cross got involved, encouraging the folks back home to "Knit Your Bit," supplying civilians with gray and khaki yarn and patterns for socks and sweaters and fingerless wristlets my grandfather and his tentmates could use to stay warm and dry Over There, as well as stump socks for amputees. The Junior Red Cross encouraged girls and boys both to "Knit for Victory," giving them simple assignments like washcloths. Every few weeks, as my grandfather's unit waited for the weather to turn and the stalemate to break, another crate arrived. The men emptied it, grateful to have not just more protection against the cold but something from home.

Not all wars are fought abroad. Right after World War II, during the Jewish uprising against the British Mandate in Palestine, while they were living underground in Tel Aviv, Menachem Begin's wife Aliza knitted. While he commanded the revolutionary group the Irgun from their small apartment, she crocheted booties and hats for their new baby, like any young mother. Begin himself never left the flat, but every day, no matter the weather, Aliza loaded their daughter into a buggy and pushed her around the block. Invariably she'd stop on the sidewalk and let some neighbor lean in to admire the child, maybe coo to her and tickle her chin before slipping a hand under the layers of blankets Aliza had spent her cloistered hours making to find Begin's coded orders to his soldiers.

Guile, forbearance, meticulousness. Waiting for Odysseus to return, Penelope pretends to be weaving a funeral shroud for his father, Laertes. When she finishes, she promises, she'll let the suitors know which one of them she's chosen, but every night, while they're sleeping off the evening's wine, she unravels the shroud so that, like Scheherazade, she can never finish.

Knitting takes time and patience, and—Madame Defarge notwithstanding—is traditionally seen as domestic and benign, which is why it's both a perfect activity and perfect metaphor for those who sit and wait. It's not merely something useful to do to bide the time. With its calm, methodical progress, it's a promise, in the midst of war and chaos and loss, that, somewhere, an orderly world still exists. A finished piece of knitting is personal—intimate in the way a favorite pair of socks or mittens is beloved. The person who knitted this for you cares. That recognition is why knitting something for someone else is so fulfilling. Whether solitary or communal, knitting is a gift that's as much a comfort to the giver as the recipient.

Surely the Germans in the trenches my grandfather watched through his field glasses were wearing socks and mufflers and gloves knitted by people they loved, and by strangers hoping to bring them some comfort. It's not sentimental to believe the Russians knitted for their troops in World War II, or the Chinese for theirs in the Korean War. The promises we make don't change. Even now our soldiers are in the mountains of Afghanistan fighting a war that seems endless. If you have the time and some extra yarn hanging around, think about knitting a hat or scarf or helmet liner for The Ships Project or one of the many sites online that connect civilians and soldiers. It gets cold up there in the Hindu Kush, and they could use something warm from home.

The Yarnery
840 Grand Avenue #2
Saint Paul, MN 55105
(651) 222-5793
www.yarnery.com

STONEHAVEN STOLE AND SCARF

designed by Theresa Gaffey

MATERIALS

For scarf: 1 skein each of 5 colors of Brooklyn Tweed Loft (275 yards per 50-gram skein). Color A (Snowbound), Color B (Sweatshirt), Color C (Almanac), Color D (Fossil), Color E (Faded Quilt)

For stole: 2 skeins each of 5 colors of Brooklyn Tweed Loft (275 yards per 50-gram skein). Color A (Hayloft), Color B (Meteorite), Color C (Plume), Color D (Fauna), Color E (Sap)

Size 6 (4 mm) needles or size needed to obtain gauge

Tapestry needle

GAUGE

20 stitches and 34 rows = 4 inches

FINISHED DIMENSIONS

Scarf: 12 inches wide and 79 inches long

Stole: 24 inches wide and 79 inches long

TO KNIT

With Color A, cast on 59 (122) stitches.

Row 1: K2, p1, (k8, p1) 6 (13) times, end row with k2.

Row 2: P2, k1, (p8, k1) 6 (13) times, end row with p2.

Repeat these 2 rows throughout, changing color as listed in stripe sequence.

STRIPE SEQUENCE

36 rows with Color A

36 rows with Color B

12 rows with Color C

36 rows with Color D

36 rows with Color E

12 rows with Color C

Repeat stripe sequence 4 times.

End with 36 rows Color A and 36 rows Color B.

TO FINISH

Bind off all stitches. Weave in ends. Block gently.

an open letter to all my unfinished projects

CLARA PARKES

The author has a long overdue talk with her fuzzy friends.

Wake from your slumber, my fuzzy friends. It's time we had a talk.

You lounge about the house, content to mooch off my good tote bags, your cast-on edge dangling ever so suggestively from the beginning of your first row. You monopolize every spare set of needles I own, often for years, nay, decades. And for what?

Have you ever once thought about my needs?

We started off so well, you and I. How beautiful the limerence of our first few rows together, the speeding ahead on the open road, wind in our hair, no burdens or baggage, just a limitless future ahead. I pictured us living a happy life together long after that final bind-off.

Where did we go wrong?

I'm talking to you, that basketball-sized bundle of hand-dyed yarn with which I cast on a Rhinebeck sweater just six days before the festival, back when I actually thought I could complete a sweater in six days. And you, that boatneck Adrienne Vittadini sweater begun in 1999 before I understood how challenging black yarn is to knit. And *you*, that heathered brown Alice Starmore pullover with the exquisite center cable motif I only worked once before setting aside. I thought I was the kind of person who would finish you, I really did.

There you all sit, my personal museum of accumulated optimism. You've been permanently frozen in place at the very moment the relationship grew tedious, before the sameness set in. Was that what happened? Did I just get bored with you?

Boredom isn't a word knitters like to use. It's like a woman admitting hunger on a first date. Only once we've finished our project, as we unfold our masterpiece and reveal millions of stitches to the world, are we ever allowed to say, "Well, the bind-off got a little . . . boring."

Admitting boredom mid-project is heresy, for it would reveal that the glorious feeling of yarn slipping through our fingers, that satisfying sight of stitch upon stitch building in our completed fabric, the joyous meditative process of knitting itself isn't enough. We can still feel ennui.

How I envy those people who remain faithful to each project from beginning to end. They are the long-distance runners of our knitting world, trotting ahead for miles and miles, overcoming heat and fatigue and that voice in their head that says, "You know, you could just stop." Or, worse yet, the one that says, "Hey, look at that skein over there. Isn't she pretty?"

These serial monogamists bring a new sweater to their knitting group every month, a new shawl, a new baby blanket, an advent calendar containing twenty-five charming, completely unique miniature knitted ornaments. They finished it so early that they may make another to give away.

I imagine their homes to be spotless, their children trained to put all their toys away at the end of each day. They've probably never needed a filling or a crown. Their desks are immaculate, they iron their sheets, and I bet they've even taught the cat how to clean its own litter box.

Except that I know this isn't true. One moment in Pasadena took the last bit of that pompous wind right out of me.

I was halfway through my first book tour, and Elizabeth Gilbert was scheduled to sign just a few hours after me. "Don't worry," a staffer told me, "we put her in the big room."

The crowd was decent, though it didn't fill the conservative number of chairs they'd set out for me. I gave my talk, trying to block that voice in my head (the same one that tries to tell me I'll never finish what I'm knitting) that was counting the people in the room and trying to tell me I was a failure.

A beautiful young woman came up to me afterwards with her book for me to sign. I was half listening, half signing, when she told me that her son had recently been diagnosed with a violent emotional disorder. I looked up, and her voice cracked as she said, "Knitting is the only thing in my life that I feel like I can control."

Which may be the real reason why we knit, isn't it? Not so much for a sweater or hat but for the rare gift of being able to create order out of chaos, something out of nothing. The world was crumbling around her, but Madame Defarge steadily knit on, stitch by stitch, forming her own army of footmen ready to do her bidding.

Maybe that's my problem. If stitches are indeed our footmen, if they expect us to command, if they actually crave a steady hand to keep them in line, I'm doomed. I am a terrible manager of people.

The second I hear my voice telling someone what to do, all I can think is, "Well aren't *we* Miss Fancy . . . Who are *you* to order another person around?" I immediately add a laugh, a joke, anything to try and grab that wisp of authority out of the air and stuff it back into my pocket. As a result, not much gets done.

My brother likes to say that my family puts the lowercase *p* in passive-aggressive. When a new neighbor started slamming her door so hard that my floor shook, I didn't go downstairs and ask her to stop. But I did briefly put her packages upside down in our entryway so she'd have to take the extra step of flipping them over to see if they were hers. *That'll show her.*

Eventually I moved out.

And so perhaps it does make sense for me to have closets and shelves and bins of unfinished projects, each paused at the exact moment I sensed an impending mutiny. Instead of ruling with an iron fist, I simply put you away.

To this day you remain in your bins and bags, like pound puppies waiting to be adopted. Sometimes I'll actually stop, pull you from your bag, and try to figure out where we went wrong. Occasionally you're just a blocking and darning away from completion. But more often than not, a cursory glance tells me we are beyond hope, that you represent a character weakness I am still not ready to face.

Do you hold grudges? Will I awake one night to discover you've taken up pitchforks and torches and are marching toward me, zombielike, seeking revenge?

If I were a better ruler of stitches, I would bravely put you out of your misery right now. I try not to think how you'd feel, my dear slumbering projects, to awaken to that brusque sensation of needle slipping from your grasp. Would it hurt, the brutal tug of your tail, or the irretrievable loss of loops within loops within loops as row by row I pull your stitches free?

Like stepping off the bridge, would we both feel regret as you fell through the air? No. At that moment you expect to hit the water, when all has unraveled, there would be no fatal SPLAT. Instead, the ultimate reincarnation would be at hand. You'd feel no pain, no regrets, just the freshness of new beginnings.

And this time, it would be different. I promise.

why i don't knit

JODI PICOULT

*Why learn to knit when you have a grandmother
like the author's who knits for you?*

I DON'T KNIT.

I am endlessly impressed by people who know how to turn
the heel of a sock, who can take circular needles and create
something linear. At farmers' markets, I gravitate toward the
booths with women who have spun and dyed their own sheep's
wool into the striated colors of the rainbow. I've gazed at the x's
and o's in pattern books the way I used to scrutinize calculus problems, as if clarity would surely come if I just stared long enough.

My aversion to knitting grew from a lack of necessity. When I
was growing up, my grandmother made my sweaters. There were
roll-necks and fisherman sweaters and delicate cardigans, fringed
ponchos and turtlenecks and sleeveless vests. They had popcorn
stitches and fringe and cables as thick as my fist. Some were itchy
as hell, and some were as soft as butter against my skin. My grandmother would visit us and sit on the couch at night as we gathered
to watch *M*A*S*H* or *Little House on the Prairie*. In the interstitial
space when the dialogue on the television stopped, before the
commercial began, I could hear her knitting needles chatter like

teeth. Her hands were smooth and dry and warm, the nails cut short, the yarn looped around her fingers. Her stitches, lined up on the metallic needles like little kamikaze pilots, would leap into the abyss between the tips one at a time, making the sacrifice of the individual to be part of the greater whole. On her lap, that scroll of wool grew by inches every time I remembered to look. Her knitting bag, a brown seventies zigzag of tapestry, squatted on its crossed haunches beside her feet. Inside were the most magical contraptions: giant safety pins to hold stitches, pattern books marked with the careful chicken scratch of her handwriting, and Ziploc bags filled with the disembodied parts of sweaters: a triangle that would be an arm, a flat square of belly, the yawning notch of a neckline. Sifting through them was like digging through a graveyard; my grandmother was the brilliant doctor who could stitch them together into their fashionable whole.

To say I idolized my grandmother would be an understatement. She took care of me when I was tiny and my mother was finishing her student teaching. She would drive me to nursery school, where she taught, and afterward, we would stop at Baskin-Robbins for ice cream. We sat on the stoop of her Bayside, Queens, apartment, peeling the paper from our cones. I would lie on her bed and watch her do her makeup, ending with an explosive dust of powder on her face, while I sifted through a button box, trying to find matches, or sorting them by color, or digging for my favorite—a pink mother-of-pearl. She kept chocolate Kisses in a crystal candy dish on the coffee table and her kitchen always smelled of detergent. She read to me, walked with me, pushed me on the swings, and clapped at my little-girl dances. My crayon drawings covered her refrigerator and my first published poem was printed in the newsletter that went out to her neighborhood in Bayside. She was one of my first fans, and definitely my most ardent one. And in return, I was hers. I watched her hands fly, as if her fingers were having a conversation, as she knit every night. I scoured the dated pictures in the knitting magazines, pointing to the sweaters I thought were prettiest. I tried on her necklaces and her snap-on earrings. I stood beside her as she carved roast chicken for dinner, sharing the peel of crispy skin as if it were our secret. I ate chocolate ice cream exclusively, because that was her favorite. My grandmother was smart, strong, beautiful, creative, talented. I wanted to be just like her.

She had been raised in the countryside of upstate New York. The daughter of immigrants, she was one of five children. She told me about her sister Frieda, who had the most magical skill— she could look at a dress on any model or in a fashion magazine, and could cut a pattern on her own and re-create the dress perfectly. My grandmother said Frieda made her the most beautiful clothing—that everyone at school was always jealous of how fashionable her outfits were. Frieda taught my grandmother to sew, and indeed, she made much of my mother's clothing when they were growing up and money was tight. She'd made matching outfits for me and my mother, when I was a baby. When I was cast as Eliza Doolittle in my middle school musical, she crafted the most stunning emerald velvet evening gown. I did not just feel like a leading lady, as I wore it to greet a preteen Henry Higgins. I felt like a princess.

It was Frieda who also taught my grandmother how to knit. By the time I had a conscious understanding of my grandmother's unerring talent with knitting needles, I had already been the recipient of her sweaters for years. Every baby photo of me that was taken in winter also features her handiwork. My school photographs almost always included a cardigan she'd made for me, or a pullover that matched my green eyes. The photograph I took

my freshman year in college, sent to my distant high school boyfriend in an effort to remind him to love me, was of me wearing an oatmeal-colored crew neck she had knit that made me look
preppy, if not provocative. (It didn't work out. Blame my naïveté,
but not my wardrobe.)

My grandmother's name is Bess, and she married Hal Friend,
giving her a moniker no one ever forgets. "Bess Friend?" people
exclaim when they meet her. "Really?" It was her leading sally at
the hospital where she volunteered for forty years, and it put ner-
vous patients at ease. One of her assignments was working in the
ward where cancer patients came for chemo. There, she knit a hat
for a patient who had lost her hair. And then another. Eventually,
she created a program at the hospital where every incoming chemo
patient received a beanie from a willing, compassionate knitter.

I remember when my grandmother first made a sweater for the
man who would become my husband—a thick, off-white cable-
knit sweater that he still has, almost twenty-five years later. If my
grandmother knit a sweater for someone outside of the immedi-
ate family, it meant that the boundary was broken; that they were
now in the inner sanctum. It was her way of saying that I'd chosen
well. I had four different sweaters for my first unborn son, sus-
pended between layers of tissue paper, months before he arrived
in this world. The sweaters she knit for my children—bright and
cozy, with polar bears and pandas and puppies on the front—were
passed down from oldest to youngest. And even though the last
of the baby clothes has long since been donated to charity, there
is still a box in my attic where those sweaters she knit now sit
between layers of tissue paper, years before my grandchildren
arrive in the world.

I never learned to knit because I didn't have to; because the
presence of my grandmother in my life, and the gifts spun from

her hands, seemed timeless and eternal to me. As the family expanded, we took turns—it might not be every birthday we received a new sweater, but every third year. Instead of a sweater, it might be a hat or a pair of socks. As my grandmother grew older, we had to take the pattern books to the copy store to enlarge the typeface and the charts, so that she could read them. Her hands, still strong-knuckled and firm, became arthritic. It got harder for her to hold the knitting needles. Sometimes she would fall asleep in the middle of a television program, in the middle of a stitch. Eventually, when she came to visit, she no longer brought the tapestry knitting bag with her.

I wondered, then, if she missed the weight of the needles in her hands. If it felt strange to stare directly at the television, instead of looking up from the work she was doing. I wondered if she yearned to smooth out the pieces of a sweater on the bare, scrubbed surface of the kitchen table, and pin them into finished form. I wondered if she touched the yarn she'd never had the chance to use and dreamed of scarves, of mittens, of wraps and pullovers that might have been, if her body had not failed her.

My grandmother is one hundred years old, now. Her joints, the first part of her physique to betray her, have not been the last. Eyes, ears, neck, stomach; she has been leaving us by degrees for several years. This week, I rush to the hospital to see her. Sitting at her bedside, I hold her small, cool hand in mine—the bones as fine and light as a bird's. Loopy with drugs, certain she is in her own home, she points at bare walls and tells me where she bought those paintings, and why she loves them. Eventually, wrapped in the arms of Tylenol 3, she drifts asleep.

I do not let go, and in that moment, I remember the one time—the *only* time—I ever attempted to knit.

I was in high school, and I was working as a lifeguard at a rest home. Occasionally I had to wade into a shallow pool to help an addled elderly lady in a swim cap festooned with plastic flowers, who had forgotten where the steps were to exit. But most of the time, I sat by myself, trying not to pass out from the chlorine fumes, bored to tears. Inspired, I decided to ask my grandmother to teach me how to knit.

What do you want to make? she asked.

A sweater.

She gave me a pair of her needles, and a skein of yarn—a ropy, rooty brown that looked like the Midwest as seen from an airplane. She offered me a pattern that she didn't think would be too difficult. She showed me how to cast on, and how to knit and purl. She taught me how to drop a stitch. She did this all quickly, like a choreographer intentionally moving fast to weed out those mentally unprepared to be challenged. But I was determined. I followed her lead, and when I didn't know what I was doing, I fudged it, creating little Swiss cheese holes in the weave.

But I didn't care, because I was going to be the most prolific knitter in the world. I was going to finish this sweater so fast it would make everyone's head spin—and it would make my grandmother swell with pride. After just two weeks, I laid on the kitchen table the two sleeves, the front and the back. I joined them together with my grandmother's help, and then, grinning, pulled the completed sweater over my head.

One sleeve ended at my elbow. The other dangled several inches past my hand. The front and the back of the sweater were not equally matched, either. There were gaps in some spots and knots in others. The sweater bunched weirdly underneath my armpits, yet also somehow gaped at the waist. It would have been perfect, if I were Quasimodo.

What do I do? I asked my grandmother.

She shrugged. *You rip it out,* she said. *And start again.*

I don't know what happened to that abomination, although I can tell you that I did not pull the stitches and begin anew. I couldn't bear to see all those months of work negated into a crimped tangle of yarn again. I had not realized that it wasn't just the mechanical act of knitting I'd have to learn. It was an evenness of tone and temper; a measure of patience. I would have to understand that it wasn't the speed with which I reached the last row, but the care with which I'd crafted each stitch.

My grandmother, maybe, had learned this lesson when her sister Frieda was her teacher. I wasn't there to see her stumble; I only arrived when she was a pro. And all my life, really, I'd followed her example. To fail at something she could do so fluently—literally, with her eyes closed—was something I could not bear.

So I didn't try again. Instead, I just gratefully accepted the birthday sweaters and the holiday scarves, continuing to take them—and my grandmother—for granted.

But as I sit at her hospital bed, I realize I should have ripped apart that sweater and started over. I should have begged my grandmother to teach me how to keep the stitches fine and the spaces even as a heartbeat. I should have heard what she had been trying to tell me all along: that what you make with your own hands is not crafted from wool, but from love.

When she could no longer knit, I should have taken up her needles.

I would have liked to make a blanket for her.

She has kept me warm for years; I only wish I could return the favor.

creation myth

ROBIN ROMM

As she knits a baby blanket for her friend's baby, the author
pauses and puts it away. What is keeping her from finishing it?

I LEARNED TO KNIT FROM MY GRANDMOTHER, A RETICENT
and withdrawn woman with dyed blond hair and piercing blue
eyes. Her emotions generally ran the gamut from flatness to
worry; I rarely saw her show abandon or excitement. But when I
was about nine, she sat with me during a visit to Eugene, teaching me to cast on, knit and purl. The speed at which I learned
and the dexterity of my small, nimble fingers opened a window to
another grandmother, one I hadn't known before. As I sat next to
her, working on a wobbly square of blue acrylic, she exhibited a
rare joy and pride.

"Look," I remember her crowing to my mother, her daughter-
in-law the trial lawyer, holding up the lumpy blue "doll blanket."
My mother nodded; totally not her cup of tea, knitting. She went
on reading a brief, planning a vacation, tolerating the visit with
her husband's difficult family. But her lack of enthusiasm didn't
dampen my grandmother's. "Look at how even your stitches are!"
she said. "So tight and straight. You're a natural, better than I am
already!"

It felt novel, nice to see her eyes shining. The act of creating something had dispelled her sadness, and I made a mental note—one that I didn't yet understand, but that I would revisit later in life. When she returned to Brooklyn, I attempted to keep going. But I was just a kid, and soon knitting fell by the wayside, lost to friend drama, reading novels, and learning how to spray up my bangs. Somehow, though, the movements and stitches became muscle memory. About six years later, in high school, I took it up again.

It started with a trip to Nepal; I had the good fortune, when I was sixteen, of getting into a summer exchange program in Kathmandu. Strolling through the markets with other exchange students, I came across a merchant selling yarn in wild colors and textures. I chose dozens of skeins, returning to buy even more, and came home with a nose piercing, glass bangles, a sari and a duffel bag of this thread—fuchsia and gold and moss green, some of it with metallic strands woven through it, some of it bound with shreds of velvet. You couldn't find anything like it in yarn stores in Oregon, and it made me want to knit. This wild, saturated fiber had mirrored Kathmandu, and had jibed with my deep love of color and texture, a love I'd taken to expressing through vintage dresses and tie-dyed leggings, costume jewelry, patchwork satchels. I knit myself rainbow-colored socks and hats and scarves. I signed up for a fiber arts class, taught by the hippie high school art teacher, and learned to spin my own wool, dying it with onion skins and lichen I picked off the trees. My mother's friend, who had llamas, brought me wool in giant garbage bags. I learned to card it, to turn it into my own version of the Nepalese yarn, and I made all manner of insane-looking hats that I wore, proudly, everywhere, much to my mother's chagrin. (She still hadn't gotten over the nose piercing.)

When I went off to college, I got busier, and I more or less stopped knitting, but in my late twenties, when my mother became terminally ill, I took it up again with a vengeance. Those hard days in the house, waiting for the inevitable which took weeks, then months, then years to come, I knit a cashmere poncho, a mohair shawl, three scarves, six sets of fingerless gloves, a cashmere baby sweater, socks for everyone, velvet hats for my dying mom. I knit and I knit and I knit as if by knitting I could somehow channel all my grief and rage and hurt and fear and manage it somehow. I never wear any of the knitted clothes I made during that time—not even the gray poncho which is truly beautiful. But I keep them folded in a box. They feel special for having survived with me. Along with writing, which I also did as if my very existence depended on it, the knitting countered the destruction. Creation to counter sadness, the lesson I'd learned from my grandmother.

And then, after the decade of losing my mother came to its awful close, I found myself in my thirties, teaching full-time, writing and publishing. I began to get invited to writing conferences and academic events and knitting offered me a way of extending my attention span and patience. If my hands were busy in some beautiful texture, if bright hand-dyed wool slid through my fingers, I was less likely, in a long faculty meeting, to scowl at the professor in love with his own vining thoughts on a fine point in a draft of a memo about computer lab use. Knitting kept me chill and serene. The repetitive physical movement actually helped me pay attention. My early thirties was also when most of my friends began to have babies. So I used these meetings and readings to make booties and stuffed knitted rabbits and the cutest cardigans you ever laid eyes on.

A few summers ago, at a writing conference, I began to knit a blanket for my friend Marika's new baby. I'd chosen brilliant hues of organic cotton: magenta, orange, violet, green, and a zigzag chevron pattern. And so I sat in a folding chair, listening to the readings and lectures under the bright Tahoe sun, letting the blanket grow and grow.

"It's beautiful," said several fellow writers. They stopped to feel the cotton between their fingers. "Who's it for?"

I'd tell them.

"I wish I had a friend like you!" one of them said. "Do you take orders?"

MARIKA AND I became friends the year after I graduated from college. She was smart (a graduate student in neuroscience), chic (raised in Manhattan), and tightly wound, prone to migraines and devastating—and devastatingly funny—takedowns of cultural phenomena.

She wore mostly silks and cottons in colors that blended with her ivory skin and set off her black hair. She had very few pieces of clothing, all of it designer and well cared for, hung properly and ironed. She despised the gaucheness of frivolous consumerism. When she made a purchase, it was a curatorial decision. She made *investments*—one gray lambskin handbag, carried for many years, two pairs of jeans she'd wear everywhere. Her bedroom in San Francisco had a bed with light gray blankets and a dark leather chair, a bookshelf with glass doors and a vintage dresser. That was it. In this minimalist environment, her hair dryer in the corner looked like a piece of Warhol inspired art. When she got pregnant and bought a small apartment in Manhattan, with her husband, she decorated it in white. White walls, white furniture, white counters, white towels.

If you haven't gathered by now, I'm more of a maximalist. My bedroom is a mess of colors: blue and coral and yellow and pink. I collect odd animal figurines and get sentimentally attached to all my sweaters, leading them to live subpar lives crammed in overflowing drawers. I didn't really consider this difference between us when I chose my colors for the blanket. The jewel tones looked beautiful to me—busy and bright. My own mother had decorated my baby bedroom in green and orange, having read that it would stimulate my mind. When I was a teenager, I painted my bedroom ceiling yellow and the walls tangerine with large white daisies all over it. I wear purple glasses and have about five pairs of red shoes. If I had a baby, I'd drape her in wild colors, get her magenta jackets and an orange hat. What's life for, anyway? It's not for wearing beige!

But as I knit, as the blanket became more and more colorful, I began to feel reluctant. Another friend at another conference stopped me to admire it. I told her I was having second thoughts about my color choices. I'd picked gender-neutral ones, but beyond that I'd just gotten what I liked. Maybe I should have given it more thought. "My friend is really chic. She only likes neutral colors," I explained. "I bet the baby's room will be all white and light gray and this blanket will look clownish."

"Well, God," said the friend, "then you totally owe it to the baby. Give that baby some color!"

With that, I forged ahead. For Marika, I told myself. For the potentially color-starved baby. In tribute to my mother's idea that bright colors would stimulate a baby's mind.

I'd recently spent many months on another baby sweater, a gift for an editor of mine, Alexis, who'd recently given birth. I hadn't meant to sink quite so much time into it, but the sweater—a turquoise kimono-style cardigan in a silk yarn—was more difficult than I had anticipated, with I-cords and special seaming. One of the sleeves had not come out the same as the other, and I'd needed to frog it. And the I-cord wove into a side hole so that it became a belt, but about this, the pattern got opaque.

Alexis received the sweater, wrapped in tissue paper and ribbons. She sent me back photos of the baby smiling inside of it. Soon after this, she was unceremoniously fired from the publishing house where I'd worked with her. I visited her at her apartment, on a work trip to New York, and got to see the baby, Otis, wearing the sweater—the silk now pilled and frayed, but the baby riotously happy that he belonged to a world with such great moms and sweaters.

"I love the sweater so much," Alexis said, fingering the broken-down fibers; and I could see that she really did, that it had made her feel a particular way to see Otis wearing it—a sweater made for her by one of her authors, part of a career she'd loved and lost, through no fault of her own, to motherhood; a creative project she'd inspired, that she could touch and wash and bring to the park. A created thing that helped stave off sadness, yet again.

I had Alexis's happiness to go on, as well as the happiness of many other recipients of handmade baby gear. And still, as I knit the blanket, I found myself pausing. Was it the color I was pausing over? Or was it something else? When I finally finished it, I wrapped the blanket in tissue paper and left it sitting in a pile by the front door. It sat there for a week. Then, cleaning the house for a dinner party, I moved it to my bedroom. It sat on the dresser for a few more weeks. Then months. Then I finally picked it up, took off the tissue paper, and put it in my closet.

THE TRUTH WAS, as I knit that blanket, as the colors slipped through my fingers, as the blanket grew, I spent more and more time imagining all the things I would knit for a baby if the baby were, indeed, mine. Blankets like that one, yes. Booties and hats, of course. But also sweaters—striped sweaters and pullovers and kimono sweaters. Little tiny cardigans styled after old-man sweaters. Sweaters with animals in their patterns. If it were a girl, sweater dresses. My mind spun out these images—the tiny sleeves, the little hems, and the feeling of slipping these over small, warm baby arms. But it wasn't the objects themselves that had me here in this fantasy for hours. It was the feeling I would have while knitting them, the anticipation of new life, of my own child arriving to change my path in ways I couldn't even imagine, the warmth and excitement of that. The fantasy would open up and haze out and soon I would be thinking up baby names, envisioning time spent outside on the lawn in the sun with an umbrella to shield her baby skin, her baby nose.

I TRY VERY hard to rise above my envy. I'm a writer, and if I gave into every feeling of envy—every award a friend wins, or every million-dollar book deal, I'd basically be a gnarled, crippled troll. I applaud the good fortune of others and I genuinely mean it. But I haven't been able to have a baby of my own, not after years of trying, and there's something different about baby envy. No matter how hard you applaud for others, you can't really drown it out. And I'll just admit that the applause starts to lose its sincerity after a while—not on the writing front, but definitely on the baby front. It just seems so unfair. I know this is a useless rueful thought; the world is unfair in ways far larger than this. But, still, it's painful.

And though I didn't really want to admit it, it was my own baby envy that made me pause. Not only did it seem that Marika wouldn't want a baby blanket knit in the gypsy, hippie hues of my Eugene childhood, it also seemed that my baby—my future baby that I could not seem to have, despite many, many attempts—would appreciate the blanket. In fact, as those needles clicked together and the blanket grew and grew, I started suspecting that perhaps I could lure it into being, this baby. If I left the blanket out for her, for him, she or he might come into my life to grab it. I pictured this blanket in a crib in a house we would have together: me, my partner Don, this baby. I don't know that it felt quite this lucid. I didn't actually have this articulate a thought. I just knew that I felt proprietary over the blanket, that the blanket was leading me deeper inside of myself and my own wishes, that it felt better to hold on to it, that it made me feel closer to a future I wished would be mine.

It felt, in some bizarre way, like an admission of defeat to send it off. And so I never did.

This was a couple of years ago. Marika is now pregnant with her second child. Many of my friends have been moms a long time. All of us are in our late thirties now, and I still haven't been successful. I've started shelling out the big bucks for the fancy doctors, and we have appointments scheduled with an adoption agency, too. I'm on medication and schedules and by the end of the year, maybe that blanket will finally find its baby.

The future isn't mine to know.

Last night, casting about for a craft project, I dug into my yarn stash and began to unravel a half-finished baby tunic I'd started for another friend's second child. "I'm not knitting for babies anymore, not unless it's our baby," I said to Don. "Then I will knit this cashmerino up into the greatest pair of infant sweater pants that ever hit America."

He looked up from his reading and said, "With you as a mom, our baby will be very well dressed."

I put the seafoam cashmerino back in the bag and zipped it closed. Knitting can be creation in the face of sadness; that's worked many times for me, for my grandmother, for friends. But I want to knit for a different reason now. I want to create for creation itself. It seems like a wonderful plot twist. Wish me luck.

sarah with an h

BILL ROORBACH

*The author joined the knitting club at Ithaca College to get
over a broken heart and meet girls. But when he met Sarah
with an H, his world turned even more upside down.*

I WAS LONELY AT ITHACA COLLEGE AFTER MY HIGH SCHOOL
sweetie dumped me for a boy who'd stayed home, 1971. And
of course after that and so young I looked for love in all the
wrong places. Bars, particularly, as the drinking age in New York
State was a near-fatal eighteen at the time. And because I played in
bands. You hear a lot about groupies but the truth is that the girls
you actually wanted to meet weren't the girls who'd walk up to
the stage and ask about your axe. Axe was slang for instrument, I
guess I'd better say. No, not those girls.

At the dentist I surreptitiously picked up an (I think) *Esquire*
magazine because there was an article touted on the cover: "Ten
Foolproof Ways to Meet Women Who Will Actually Like You."
The tips were humorous, mostly, and pretty unexceptional, but
one was "Take a dance class." I wasn't going to do that—I'd taken
dance all through high school. Another was something about
church. Church? Not me. The tip that stayed with me was to join
a club, one that men didn't usually join. Their example was a gar-

den club. I liked gardening just fine, but I knew that joining the Garden Club would be a better way to meet my mother than any possible lover.

The lonely weeks went by. Then in Egbert Student Union one day, after having a beer at the pub (yes, we had a pub in the Student Union, and it opened at 8 a.m.—a different era), I spotted a mimeographed flyer, and then saw it all over campus:

COLLEGE KNITTING CLUB FORMING!!!

I thought the three exclamation points were pretty funny, an attempt to create excitement where there was unlikely to be much. But an idea took hold. My grandmother had always knitted and I had always loved holding the yarn for her while her needles clattered away. She was a production knitter, my grandma, and had kept eight children and then thirty-six grandchildren in hats and sweaters and mittens and muffs. She also told great stories. One was that a horse had stepped on her cousin Molly when the poor kid was only eight—this would have been in 1895 or so—and crushed her face, creating a permanent, grotesque disfigurement. The rest of the story was about Molly's eventual wedding to a perfectly normal fellow, and her nest full of perfectly normal kids.

I called the number on the poster, a campus number, and thought it was pretty auspicious that the young woman who answered was also named Molly. Yes, she said, with three exclamation points after every phrase, the club was shaping up with three members already!!! It hadn't ever come up whether they took boys, but why not!!!

So that next Sunday afternoon when all the boys I knew were watching football, I slipped over to Hilliard Hall, which was a girls' dorm. Parietal rules had just been lifted, and it felt very transgressive to just march right in. Each dorm had a big lounge outfitted with couches and easy chairs and in Hilliard Lounge I found not the three women Molly had mentioned but *nine*, and every single one of them had a big carpetbag full of hanks and balls and skeins of yarn and bristling with knitting needles. And I can tell you, none of those young women had been stepped on by a horse, as far as was visible, and were of all shapes and sizes, all colors and creeds, every possible sort of hair, each head wilder than the next.

All conversation ceased, all eyes turned to me.

"You really came!!!" said Molly. She was Afro-American, as we said back then, and she was very tall and thin, with a long, slender neck, very striking, great halo of curls.

I was ready to flee, but Molly was quick to grab me, introduce me around. Two of the women pushed their easy chairs apart such that another—the last in the room—could be inserted in the circle, and there I perched.

"Well!!!" Molly said. "Let's get started!!! This is going to be a sit-and-knit kind of club!!! Let's go around and talk about our knitting experience!!!"

June was next to me. She was a woman of considerable girth and had been knitting only since the past summer on Cape Cod, she said, where her aunt had taught her a few stitches and June had found she liked doing it. She'd been acting as the au pair to her aunt's small kids, who were her own four cousins, and without the knitting, she said, she would have gone crazy. I had never heard the term *au pair* before, and had seldom thought of the loneliness of women, so already I was learning something.

There were two gals (they all said gals) named Patricia, soon to be Pat and Patty. Patty was the most conventionally good-looking of the women, what you might call a hottie today. She said she knitted for Jesus. I knew that meant she wouldn't be knitting for the likes of me.

There were two gals named Sarah, one of them to become known as Sarah with an H. And Sarah with an H, well, there was just something about her. She had been knitting since she was a little girl, she said. And modestly, she declared herself an expert, and willing to teach us all anything she could. Molly added a large number of exclamation points to that offer. Sarah's sweater was dazzling, knit from something soft across the shoulders and bust, but knit from something harder and darker in the arms and belly, with a half-fringed hem, all pieced beautifully to flow into her very short skirt, which she'd also knitted, along with her very long knitted stockings, a bit of sleek thigh peeking out. Her clogs were thick felt, and I was surprised when she said she hadn't made them. She talked about mitten patterns and crazy hats she'd invented and afghans the size of painter's tarps, not even a single exclamation point. She was broad-shouldered, said she was a swimmer. Her legs were long and her knees grew halfway into our circle. She kept tugging her skirt up with two hands, then smoothing it back down, tugging it up, smoothing it back down, those glimpses of thigh. Her demeanor was as soft as the bust of her sweater, whatever that material was, and her hair was like a ball of yarn, pulled tightly back, yet with long loose pieces escaping the faulty bun. She was so demure that I think it took everyone by surprise when she pulled out her current project, which looked like a small, very multicolorful sock, and announced: "I'm making my boyfriend a dick cozy."

Everyone except Jesus Patty roared with laughter, not least myself, though it made me shy to be talking about weenies, also sad: she had a boyfriend. And already I'd decided she was the girl I'd signed on for all this to meet, the one and only. I would knit my way into her heart!

When it came to my turn to speak I mentioned my grand-mother and poor, horse-stomped Molly, and that I hadn't done a whole lot of knitting beyond that.

"We will teach you," said Sarah with an H.

"I don't even have the . . . stuff," I said.

And quickly I was provided with several types of needles and several off-color balls of yarn. Jesus Patty stood up so I could sit by Sarah with an H, likely less to accommodate me than to get away from *her*.

Soon all the women were knitting away, drawing projects from their voluminous bags, and soon again I was too, knitting away, Sarah with an H reminding me of my basic stitches and even helping with my posture, her warm hand on my arm, those long legs, that soft, fuzzy bust. And the boyfriend.

That cozy she'd showed off looked awfully large to me.

MY ATTENDANCE AT the knitting club grew more and more spotty, and the conversation was no doubt better without me there in any case. But I'd made friends with Molly, and often saw her around campus, got to know some of her non-knitting friends, and my loneliness abated, if only slightly.

Home for Christmas, and several body blows: my old girlfriend with her new boyfriend at the carol sing, for one example. My old girlfriend with her new boyfriend at the Kelloggs' annual party, for another. I'd have liked to knit him a noose, but kept it civil, got a huge laugh from the happy couple when I said I'd taken up the needles.

Back at Ithaca, I really had. Sarah with an H wasn't getting along too well with Jesus Patty, so, like me, she'd only go to the club sporadically. But she was a devoted knitter and I'd sit in her little cinderblock dorm room—a rare single—and we'd knit and talk, and talk and knit, really lovely. We would listen to Joni Mitchell and knit quietly; we'd listen to Jimi Hendrix and knit intensely. She smelled like morning. Once she wriggled out of her skirt and stood there in torn blue panties and all innocently asked if the current project were the right length for a tea dress.

"Maybe a little short," I said.

And she'd bid me stand and I'd try on this or that sweater, always a little too big for me, stuff destined for her huge boyfriend, whose birthday was in March. They were going skiing spring break, and she meant to give him some good cold-weather presents.

She came to see my band play at the Salty Dog, a fairly rough place at the time. Like me, she was a bit of a loner, and turned up solo, that dress now a socially acceptable length, if still quite short. The guys wanted to know who she was and I intimated that I was seeing her. "Spend half my time in her room," I said truthfully.

She sat a table with our notebooks and extra strings and soundman and drank with him while we played. Occasionally, when no one else was, she stood up and danced, used the whole dance floor, a lot of legs, her hands shy, pulling up that hem and smoothing it down on her long thighs even as she shimmied. My heart thumped. All eyes were upon her. Sarah with an H!

She had a car, her old family station wagon, front seat like a couch. She drove me home though she said she was drunk, and in the freshman parking lot at the far top of the hill she parked and we just sat there, a last, long, lovely song on her eight-track, Neil Young's "Harvest Moon." There was a moon, and as the song ended she turned to me and said, "I wish you were my boyfriend."

"I wish, too."

"Randy is such a shit sometimes, and so far away, and here you are right here."

My heart thumped once again. I slid to her on the seat and she slid to me and we met halfway, sat shoulder to shoulder as we did knitting. Finally, I turned to her and she turned to me and we kissed very briefly, heat rising into my face.

"Better not," she said.

"One more," I said.

"Okay," she said.

And we made it a long one, slightly awkward side-by-side like that, she pulling up that hem, smoothing it down, suddenly kissing me passionately, small noises back in her throat, that morning smell. I tried pulling up the hem of her lovely knit dress and she let me get just about far enough—those sleek thighs, a certain humidity—before smoothing my hand right out of there.

"Better not," she said again.

"Better not," I repeated.

"Randy will kill me."

AFTER THAT, our knitting sessions were all suppression. We'd sit hip-to-hip on her bed for hours, she giving me instructions in her curt way and giggling over my mistakes. For a joke I'd knock Randy's photo facedown on her dresser, and definitely noticed when he wasn't put right as he had been on earlier knitting nights. I'd put my head on her shoulder, and perhaps she'd kiss my cheek, but only in farewell, and only ever so briefly.

I was trying to make an afghan of squares, but often I'd miss some crucial part of the stitch and my squares would come out as tight little triangles. Sarah said there was no reason an afghan couldn't be sewn of triangles, but when I tried to make them on purpose, I got squares again. She had me try on the newest sweater—the girl was a machine—and I noticed this one fit. We were awfully good friends. I'd stay the night, snuggle with her, the two of us always in our clothes, tangled with one another. I'd watch her sleep for what seemed hours sometimes, kiss her cheek, sniff her neck: dawn.

But the nights she came to my gigs, we'd make out in her car. At least that, which she always cut off before it got too heated, maybe a song's worth, maybe two.

Just before our spring break, she gave me that newest sweater, a boiled coral-colored one with elaborate cabling, a garment I'd have for decades to come, long after I'd last seen her.

AFTER SPRING BREAK, things were different. Sarah returned to the original knitting club. She needed friends, she said. I'd grown more uncomfortable with the club—except for Molly, none of the women had much to say to me, and I noticed that the talk died out when I arrived, or turned into a grilling: How do you stay focused on school when you're playing in that band! How much do you drink, anyway? Why is a cute boy like you sitting around with the likes of us? Like having a dozen moms.

Except Sarah, who'd closed me out entirely.

I'd had a knitting idea that hadn't come to fruition before the devastation of my friend's retreat from me after spring break, which had made it seem impossible, but now I worked on it, pretty simple: I took four of those colorful triangles from my failed afghan, sewed them together point-to-point in pairs, added some strings, and made a bikini. I should say a comic bikini, because it wasn't one a person could wear out in public, that was for sure, not with my loose stitches and poor sense of drape, just a joke, something I hoped would lighten the mood between us.

I put it in a shoe box with a couple of smooth rocks I'd found to throw her off if she shook the box, and then I wrapped it very nicely (Sunday funnies for wrapping paper, mostly "Peanuts" showing) and left it in front of her door with a "Guess who?" kind of note.

Not a peep.

Molly was in my physics class. I asked if she'd seen Sarah.

"Sarah with an H? Didn't you hear? She went home. She's been depressed, I guess. Me, I wouldn't go home if I were depressed!!! Home is where I go to *get* depressed!!!"

"I feel like an awful friend," I said. I meant, How had I not noticed?

"Well, she's going to flunk out if she's not careful!!!"

So much for compassion.

Then, not three weeks later, near the end of the semester, I looked up from my keyboard at the Salty Dog and there was Sarah with an H, dancing, not a stitch or purl of knit anything, but blue jeans like she never wore and one of those Mexican wedding shirts that were so popular, flip-flops. It was a warm night and she danced till she sweated, no particular notice of me, just dancing, dancing, tall girl, the crowd shrinking and growing around her, one of my band's best nights ever, musically speaking.

I had begun to sing a few of our songs, and the one time she caught my eye was as I was singing "Dancing in the Moonlight," which had been written by an acquaintance, Sherman Kelly, the closest I'd ever been to any famous song, and now a girl to sing it to. Not that she seemed to care.

Then she was suddenly gone.

After, the guys and I packed up the stage awhile, just the usual banter, all of us feeling pretty good about our prospects. The owner of the club had given us a bonus, unheard of. Still, I was down.

Out in the parking lot, waiting for the drummer, who was to

give me a ride, a car pulled up, huge old station wagon. Sarah, of course. With an H. "Get in, get in," she said, so urgent.

She was wearing the comic bikini, but there was nothing funny about it now. For a boy that age (or maybe any age), a girl's skin, her figure, her willingness to show you, all of that is magic greater than the magic that made the world, or maybe the same magic; anyway, she said, "I'm cold," and giggled like a brook falling down a mountain, more magic, and bid me slide close to her and, heater blasting, we drove up to that high lonesome parking lot side-by-side.

She parked, turned to me, suddenly all earnest: "Do you know what happened?" she said. "Spring break?"

"Of course I don't know what happened."

"Well, now you will. Randy had another girl there. Another girl! In another room at the ski lodge. And he was too chicken to tell either of us!"

"Is that where you've been?"

"I couldn't face anyone."

"I love your outfit."

"It itches."

And she kissed me, very hungry. And took the itchy garment off.

Magic, as I have said. And so we made love, first right there in her car, then again in her room as the sun came up, all very smoothly, as if we'd been lovers a long time. "It's always been you," she said. We cried, that's what I remember. I don't know what we were mourning. The lost months, I suppose. We professed our undying love, and that was tearful, too. We kissed till our lips were sore. Well, in the end everything was sore.

At dinner later, and after a few hours' sleep, she cried again, and really blubbering, said, "No one's ever knitted me anything."

And we had to leave the restaurant.

In her room, she put my bikini back on. It wasn't as silly as I'd thought. Maybe she'd worked on it, I don't know. But it was the most perfect fit of any tiny thing I'd ever seen.

She found a small box in her desk drawer, nicely wrapped. It looked as if it might have been there awhile.

"I knit something for you, too," she said, and handed it over.

I've had that silly cozy for decades, too, not that there's ever been any call to wear it, not after that one night, and all the laughs, and the further tears, and the thoroughgoing magic that couldn't last the summer.

Knit Purl
1101 Southwest Alder Street
Portland, OR 97205
(503) 227-2999
www.knit-purl.com

RIVULET COWL

designed by Jocelyn Okubo

SIZE
One size

FINISHED DIMENSIONS
42" circumference, 9" height

SKILL LEVEL
Easy

MATERIALS
2 skeins Trinity Worsted by SweetGeorgia Yarns
70% Merino, 20% Cashmere, 10% Silk
200 yds/115 g
Shown in Magpie

TOOLS
Size 7 (4½ mm) circular needles, 32" long
Size 8 (5 mm) circular needles, 32" long
Stitch marker
Tapestry needle

GAUGE

20 sts & 24 rnds = 4" in Bamboo Stitch Pattern, after blocking

NOTES

This pattern used to be known as the Bamboo Stitch Cowl.

Rnd 1: *YO, K2, pass yo over last two knit sts;

rep from * to end.

Rnd 2: Knit.

DIRECTIONS

Using smaller needles, CO 210 sts.

Pm and join to work in the rnd, being careful not to twist sts.

Knit 4 rnds.

Change to larger needles and work Bamboo Stitch Pattern for 8½".

Switching back to smaller needles, knit 3 rnds.

BO loosely. We suggest this method:

*k2 tog tbl, place st back on LH needle;

rep from * to last st.

FINISHING

Weave in ends. Steam block lightly to measurements.

just this

DANI SHAPIRO

*In a lifetime of lessons learned, the author learns a surprising
one after she puts her yarn away.*

S A YOUNG WOMAN, I SPENT A LOT OF TIME IN CHURCH
basements. This was a direct result of having previously
spent a lot of time in bars. I had made a mess of my life,
and had stumbled through the doors of Alcoholics Anonymous as
a lost soul, a penitent into a house of worship. Here was something I could fix; I could stop drinking. I had no idea whether
drinking was at the root of my problems, or merely a symptom,
but I was pretty sure that no one's life had ever been made worse
by getting sober.

I was living in New York City, where there seemed to be an
AA meeting on every corner. These meetings were filled with
an unlikely cross-section of life in New York: you'd see a high-
powered attorney sitting in a metal folding chair, his sleek leather
briefcase leaning against a Hefty bag stuffed with all the belongings
of a man whose home was a subway grate down the street. You'd
see former child actors; cops; schoolteachers; musicians. Everyone
had a story, and a reason to tell it. The stakes were high. In many
cases, the stakes were life and death. People had grown-up prob-

lems. Busted marriages, lost children, financial doom, ill health. Little more than a child myself, I listened hard. I felt at home, welcomed, deeply relieved to be among people who were trying to tell the truth about their lives.

One particular meeting I favored was in a church on the Upper East Side called the Church of the Heavenly Rest, which my friends and I called the Church of the Overly Dressed. It was a large, popular meeting, and the front row was taken up by women of a certain age—perhaps even the age I am now—who had been sober for decades. These women came carrying canvas tote bags from the Guggenheim or MoMA, filled with yarn of every hue. They had *projects*. An arm of a sweater might peek from a bag, a corner of a baby blanket, a long, elaborate scarf. With strong, practiced fingers they worked away, needles clicking gently, necks bent gracefully, heads bowed toward their knitting. They rarely raised their hands to share. The sense I had was that they had moved past their stories. They were more interested in listening than speaking. Whatever pain and hardship, whatever tragedy had first brought them through the doors of Alcoholics Anonymous, was well behind them, the scorched earth of a distant land. The knitting women were disciplined, gentle, elegant, and quietly warm. If one of them caught my eye, she would smile and nod in my direction, as if acknowledging a sisterhood I didn't feel I deserved.

The girl I was could not have imagined the woman I grew up to become. I suppose this is often the case. We cannot envision our future selves. *You're going to write many books, teach at a university, get married, have a baby, leave the city, move to the countryside.* The girl I was would have laughed in disbelief—or perhaps she would have recoiled in horror. After all, she had other plans. Grand, inchoate plans. *Oh, and you're going to drink again, eventually. One evening, in a candlelit restaurant, at dinner with your beloved husband, you are going to order a glass of good red wine.* No! she would have cried. Don't do it! *My darling girl, a long life is composed of chapters. Although, unlike a good novel, those chapters may not form a lovely narrative arc, or any arc at all. Don't worry. It will all be fine. It just won't be what you think.*

I hadn't thought of the knitting ladies of the Church of the Overly Dressed until I became pregnant with my second child. We were living in rural Connecticut, and it was winter. The sun set early, and nights were long and dark. Our snow-covered meadow sparkled in the light of the moon. Mornings, we would see fresh animal tracks—fox, deer, coyote—crisscrossing the fields. I was in my early forties, and the pregnancy was hard-won. My son had been very ill as an infant. We'd nearly lost him, and it had taken me a good, long while before I felt capable of even considering another child. A baby meant a ripped-open heart. A baby meant terrifying risk. We had escaped ruin, my husband, little boy, and I. Why mess with a good thing?

During those long, dark evenings, as that second baby grew inside me, I became restless, fearful. I paced the house, not knowing what to do with myself. I couldn't sit still and read. Television didn't hold my attention. I didn't want to look at my husband's hopeful face. I was desperate for something to do with my hands. My son's nanny, a Brazilian woman named Maria who is one of the calmest, wisest, and most competent people I know, had recently learned to crochet, so I asked her to teach me. At a local shop with a sign out front in the shape of a lamb, I filled a basket with skeins of yarn in baby-colors. Soft yellow, pale pink, periwinkle blue. I sat with Maria as she patiently put her hands over mine, demonstrating the most basic slipknot and chain stitch. I had no ambitions, followed no pattern. I simply made straight lines. Row after row, I stitched my way into the future. I made dozens of scarves, most of them child-sized. I imagined two boys having a snowball fight. Bunk beds. A dinner table set for four. Each time I finished one, it felt to me that I was building a soft, woolen wall, a fortress that would encircle my growing family, protect us and keep us from harm.

I knew the odds, of course. After I lost the pregnancy at fifteen weeks, I never touched those skeins of yarn again. They had served their purpose, and I was grateful for those long nights, my hands busily working by lamplight, my aluminum hook pulling loop after loop, one stitch at a time. Those hours had softened my attention, had relaxed the periphery. *Just this,* each stitch whispered. *In this life of ours, we cannot know who we will become, what will be delivered to us.* I took this lesson to heart, as I had all the other lessons. I was nothing if not a diligent student. And could I have imagined then the next chapter in this unwieldy, beautiful, chaotic thing called life? *You will love your little family of three and treat it like your greatest treasure, which, of course, it is. You will not regret this loss, though still, there will be winter nights in the future when you are pierced with a sorrow so powerful it will leave you doubled over, gasping. You will pour yourself a glass—or two, or three—of good red wine as you look out the window at the snow-covered meadow, the lone swing, your son's, now a relic of his own childhood, already gone.* The ladies at the Church of the Overly Dressed, their presence, their silence, their bowed heads, as deliberate as a row of nuns. *There's nothing else to do but this.*

ema's lessons

SAMANTHA VAN LEER

*When the author knits a scarf for her mother, she finally
understands why her great-grandmother knit.*

T HE FIRST SWEATER I EVER RECEIVED FROM MY GREAT-
grandmother was royal blue, the profile of a brown-
spotted puppy smack in the center of the chest with its
ear dangling, as if the dog were bursting through the stitches. I
proudly walked around my preschool classroom, playing with the
floppy ear, informing my classmates that my sweater was one of
a kind, made just for me by my Ema. I had watched Ema knit
my family everything from the strawberry hat that appears in
every one of my baby photos to the copious amounts of scarves
and socks she handed out on family holidays. She devoted hours
of time and energy just so we could have our personally designed
sweaters of choice.

In second grade, my extended family gathered at my house to
celebrate Hanukkah. After our traditional giant Jewish meal, we
waddled to the living room to digest and to exchange presents.
My aunt placed a gift in my lap, and I carefully snapped the tabs
of tape and peeled back the paper. Inside was my very own pair
of knitting needles and a ball of vibrant pink yarn. Holding these

simple tools, I felt empowered. I could make anything. Visions of sweaters, scarves, hats, gloves, and socks floated in my head. Excited, I showed my present to my family, and then ran up to Ema and asked if she would teach me.

After the gift-giving had concluded, Ema took me into a quiet room. She was the most wonderful knitter in the world, but as it turned out, she was possibly the worst teacher. She took my needles in her hands, which were weathered, as if each crease and mark on her skin counted the seconds she'd lived and the breaths she'd taken. But those hands were also wise, and remembered the repetitive motions of many years. She comfortably slipped the needles into position and effortlessly twisted the yarn around her finger.

"Watch carefully now," she told me as she cast a stitch at lightning speed. I strained my eyes to see her swift movements. Yet no matter how much I tried I could not decipher Ema's rapid actions. The stitches knotted tightly next to each other without a gap to be found. After she had knit three perfect, neat rows, she handed the needles to me. "Now you try. I'll be back after I frost the cakes."

Completely at a loss, I sat holding my one-fortieth of a scarf, wondering if maybe it was long enough for one of my dolls to wear. The door creaked open and in came my grandmother, smiling.

"I know Ema isn't always the best teacher . . ." she told me, taking the needles and yarn from my lap. She turned toward me so I could see her movements. "You keep this needle in your right hand, and this one in your left. Wrap the yarn around one finger, like so. Now take the tip of the needle and pick up this loop. Pull the string over, and dip your needle through, and then pull the loop off onto the other needle," Grandma instructed.

She passed me the needles and walked me through the steps again until I could do it myself without guidance. I continued to practice making lumpy, loopy rows above the three perfect sets Ema had completed.

My hands and arms ached after finishing merely four rows; I wondered how much longer it would take to create a whole scarf. The gifts I received from Ema were beautiful and flawless, but I never considered the time she spent knitting through sore fingers to make *me* the perfect sweater. After what felt like years, I walked back out to my family, proudly revealing the start of my knotted mess of a scarf.

Ema examined the stitches. "Very good! In no time you'll be making sweaters!"

Behind Ema I could see Grandma grinning. She gave me a secret nod, and I nodded back. It brought Ema so much joy to think she was able to pass this knitting skill to her only great-granddaughter, so my grandma and I kept our mouths shut, nodding along whenever Ema told the story of how she taught me to knit.

I never did finish the pink scarf. I slowly became an ADD knitter, starting one project only to cast it aside whenever I discovered a new yarn I wanted to use. I had about ten potholder-sized scarves, shamefully buried in the depths of my closet. I stuffed my knitting supplies under my bureau, where they occasionally popped out, mocking my failures.

When I was young, I didn't understand how Ema could sit tirelessly creating these works of art from start to finish. But Ema had always been a fighter. Even when she felt sick or tired she'd never show it—instead she'd put on her lipstick, blush, and a brave face, never complaining or sitting down to rest. It was this willpower that allowed her to have the discipline to knit. But as I grew older, I began to see that it was more than just persistence that drove Ema. None of these sweaters or hats or scarves had ever been for her. Every stitch she cast was for someone else. That burning flame of energy in her that never seemed to blow out was fueled by her love for others, because she knew just how happy it was going to make us when we opened those gifts. On the contrary, every project I had ever attempted was for me, and me only. I realized that to truly have my work mean something—to have that drive to finish what I started—my project had to be destined for someone else.

One year, my mom had persistently begged for an infinity scarf for Christmas. She sent emails to my brothers and me; she slipped a mention of it into the dinner conversation each night; she always oohed and aahed when we passed one in the glass windows of a shop. However, everyone in my family assumed someone else was getting her one, so no one actually did. Mom was devastated. Perhaps because I wanted to see the look on her face when she finally got one (or perhaps just to stop her complaining), I decided to knit her an infinity scarf in a single day. She was leaving the next morning for a business trip and the pressure to complete the scarf pushed me to knit till 1 a.m. My hands shook from exhaustion and I had to prop two pillows under my arms to stop them from cramping. Finishing that scarf was exhilarating, exhausting, and surreal. Giving it to her felt like handing my child to its adoptive parents. It was difficult and heartbreaking to let go of this creation I had worked so hard to make, but the look on Mom's face was priceless when she finally got the one present she'd wanted for months. She immediately put on the scarf, a smile bursting across her face when she looked at herself in the mirror. "I love it! I love it! I love it!" she kept repeating, "It's absolutely perfect!"

I didn't get to keep that physical gift of a scarf for myself, but I wasn't left empty-handed. The reward that came with the act of giving someone else the fruits of my hard labor was better than I could have imagined. As hard as it was, as tedious as the act became, as much as I ached, I couldn't give up because I wouldn't just be failing myself, but also someone I loved. As it turned out, I had been wrong about Ema getting nothing in return for those beautiful sweaters: she got love. It was knotted into every stitch, and returned to her exponentially. I get little sparks of joy every time I see my mom proudly wearing her scarf. I know every time she is complimented or catches her reflection in a mirror, she thinks of me. Ema may have struggled to teach me the basics of knitting, but she taught me something much more important: the real magic of this hobby has nothing to do with yarn; it's the ability to give back to others.

the santa stocking

LEE WOODRUFF

As children, the author and her husband had identical hand-knit Christmas stockings. All these years later, those stockings reflect a lifetime spent together.

A FEW YEARS INTO MY MARRIAGE, AWAITING THE arrival of our second child, my mother-in-law must have decided that I was in the picture to stay. "Now that you're a family," she declared over the phone, "I'm sending along some of our holiday decorations for your collection."

I imagined my husband's homespun grade school treasures; the kind of pipe cleaner reindeers and clay handprint ornaments that only a mother could love. When the box arrived, I eagerly picked through a cache of dry-clean-only snowflake table runners, and hand towels embroidered with "Noel," "Joy" and "Peace." There was a set of 1940s glass icicle ornaments that had belonged to Bob's grandmother, an elf soap dispenser and a porcelain plug-in tree with small colorful lights. But it was a knitted item, nestled at the bottom of the box, which caused my face to split into a wide grin. I was tickled to discover that my husband's handmade childhood Christmas stocking was the exact duplicate of my own.

I lifted the stocking out of the box and ran my finger over Santa's white mohair beard, plush as a Persian kitten. The name "Bob," knitted in kelly green and outlined against the red yarn, was the same number of letters as my own. In some crazy, kismet, Ouija board way, the existence of Bob's identical boyhood stocking confirmed for me what I already knew. I had found my perfect mate.

On a *Brady Bunch*-style split screen of a long-ago Christmas morning, I could picture us as grade-schoolers in Detroit, Michigan, and Albany, New York. We tug our stockings down from the brick-fronted hearths at the very same moment. Lumpy and bulging with Santa's largesse, we pull out ChapStick and Life Savers, nectarines and toothbrushes, the tangible rewards for being good girls and boys.

When I hang up those two stockings now, I cannot help but revisit the more elemental time in which they were knitted. Or is it just that every parent believes their own childhood was simpler? It is almost incomprehensible to my children when I tell them I used a typewriter in college, there were only three TV channels and something called a long-distance phone call. They are incredulous when I describe how my middle school Home Economics final included demonstrating how to crack an egg.

In the early years of the Kennedy presidency, when my great-aunt chose that popular knitting pattern, there was a universally accepted template for conduct. Character counted. A person's integrity and reputation mattered; so did humility and respecting your elders. In those days, most folks looked up to politicians. Movie stars were admired for their work, instead of their sex tapes and Twitter followings.

The coming turmoil of the Vietnam War, equal rights demonstrations and race riots had not yet begun to unravel the seams and stitches of my childhood world. They would bring the country to a boil in the later part of that decade. As the outlines of my Christmas stocking began to take shape in Aunt Esther's capable hands, the expectations for me as a wife and mother had yet to be challenged, expanded and upended. Boys grew up to be men. Girls were expected to be ladies and homemakers.

Mastering the art of knitting was but one skill among the many essential accomplishments for being a good housewife and mother. Clever girls could darn socks and sew their own clothes, but knowing how to knit was an extra bonus.

ALTHOUGH NEVER A prolific knitter herself, my mother set out to prepare her three daughters well. She had a two-thirds success rate. Try as I might, I was always on the outside of the knitting circle. Unlike my sisters, my hands were clumsy, my fingers unable to fluidly work the needles. I was (and still am) the girl with ants in her pants.

Right from the get-go, I was in it for the stuff. I loved the varying sized needles, some wood, others matte metallic colors. I coveted the half-moon set that curved to make the neck of a sweater. At Woolworth's, strolling through the yarn section I dawdled over the skeins, drawn to the loud bright colors, the tomato reds and hot pinks, the trendy tie-dyed lots, one hue melting into the next on a single strand.

My first solo project, memorable for its heinous outcome, was a scarf for my father. The end result was the size of a barn plank with a rust-golden yarn that resembled the color of old earwax. Receiving that gift with enthusiasm must have required every acting skill my father possessed. Crestfallen, I don't ever recall him wearing it, and that pretty much signaled the end of my knitting days.

It was my middle sister, Nancy, who embraced the knitting life with gusto. She became an overachiever in the category. While pregnant with her first child, she set out to knit the majority of his baby clothes; sweaters and cashmere onesies, adorable animal shaped hats and mini-mittens.

Nancy created the iconic object in our girlhood home that is still the subject of much ribbing today. It could be argued that the "Boyfriend Blanket" was knitting's greatest gift to the three teenage McConaughy girls, who, lacking a brother, were somewhat in the dark when it came to understanding the male species.

THE FULL-SIZED PURPLE and white wool throw graced the couch of our family room for more than a decade. In case the name alone isn't enough of a tip-off, the blanket, with its alternating colored squares, was perfectly sized to hide a multitude of groping teenaged sins. Let's just say that the Boyfriend Blanket saw its share of serious action in the department of lust. Perhaps it's better to just leave it at that. I can only hope that my mother occasionally thought to douse it in Woolite.

Nancy and Megan would go on to be proficient, albeit occasional knitters. When I visit my sisters' homes today, I admire the jaunty knitting bags that rest by couches or beneath bedside tables in a variety of sizes. In her living room, Nancy's perfectly arranged birch bark basket is set by the hearth like something out of an *Architectural Digest* shoot. I accuse her of staging the knobby skeins of yarn that range in hues from the Aegean Sea to cornflower blue and lapis lazuli. But then she pulls out the half-finished neck warmer she is making for a friend undergoing chemo, and I am momentarily chastened. And envious.

I will never be a knitter, just as I know that I will never take up golf. My wool gathering is carried out in other ways. And yet it still feels odd to me that the language of knitting is one I do not speak. We three sisters have always shared similar interests and hobbies. We are all avid, prolific readers, regularly swapping and discussing books. And while we swim, hike, garden, practice yoga and bake in different combinations of religiosity, when it comes to the art of knitting, as the firstborn, I am somewhat perplexed to find that I'm the one who doesn't belong.

EACH CHRISTMAS SEASON, when I lift our family stockings out of the holiday storage box, I smile as I hang them on the mantel. In the ten different houses where we have lived, overseas, on both coasts and places in between, with all of the possessions we've given away or lost, I am somewhat amazed that these two relics from Bob's and my childhood have survived.

Clichéd and cheesy as it may sound, it's hard not to think of them as a metaphor for our marriage. Although they are whole, the yarn is noticeably faded with moth holes and snags in places. Over the years those stockings have been mashed in cardboard boxes, hauled overseas, baked in the excruciating heat of multiple attics, survived a basement flooding and the assault from uncounted critters. Like the two of us, they are still hanging on, still a pair.

Early on, my husband and I put our shoulders into building a life together as Bob's journalism career took us from city to city. We had a son, and then added a daughter, got a bonus round with twin girls and moved overseas for a few years. Like every couple, we traveled smooth parts of the road and braced as we encountered the bumpier patches. Although we have journeyed together mostly in lockstep, at various junctures in our married life, we have each tasted the bittersweet fruit of adversity. There were celebrations and setbacks, triumphs, and, inevitably the losses.

When Bob was gravely injured by a bomb in Iraq, I was in my mid-forties, still a young woman with small children. Everything I had thought of as my life, my family and our sense of security, unraveled in an instant. During those days, visiting the past brought only sorrow, thinking about the future created anxiety. There was no other alternative but to learn how to stay in the present, difficult as that was to achieve at times.

OVER TIME, I would come to understand that the power to heal lay not in asking "why me" but in accepting the "why *not* me." Life is simply random, I realized, kind and cruel in equal turns. Salvation lies in making the decision to move forward.

In the year after Bob's injury, I taught myself, through gritted teeth, to stick to my knitting, to stay the course and believe that good things lay ahead. That uncertain stretch revealed the simple beauty in the endurance of the human spirit. I would learn firsthand that we are ultimately built to survive, still hard-wired to feel joy.

We were a lucky family, one that had been blessed with a miraculous recovery, but we were changed. Our priorities had been reshuffled and reorganized. We cared less about possessions and treasured more dearly the folks who formed a circle around us to knit our family back together.

That wide-eyed bride who delighted in discovering her husband's childhood stocking is now a time-tested, clear-eyed wife. But I'd like to think I am a wiser woman now, one who tries to worry less about the things I cannot control. Most days, I'm more than halfway there.

As each of our children hits adulthood, as they flutter or leap out of the nest and someday choose mates of their own, I think about the fate of Bob's and my aging Christmas stockings. What will become of those old things? What use will they be to anyone else? Who would want them? And yet I cannot now imagine parting with them, tossing them into a clothing donation bin or putting them out with the trash.

IN THE END, I recognize that none of the physical objects we leave behind will define us. I hope that we will leave our imprint in other ways. I want us to be remembered as a family that loved well and gave of ourselves; that tried hard and looked outward and attempted to move through the world with grace. We nurtured and were, in turn, nurtured back. For that, I have nothing but gratitude.

the art of losing

ANN HOOD

Facing a new change in her life, Ann Hood rediscovers the
healing power of knitting.

W HEN YOUR MARRIAGE IS FALLING APART, YOU
walk around every day feeling like you are at the
edge of something—a windowsill, a rooftop, a
cliff—barely hanging on. Every time you look at your children
you lose your breath, not in the usual way, which is to say that
gasp mothers feel at how marvelous their kids are, how smart and
funny and perfect. No, you lose your breath because you worry
you are about to ruin everything for them. No more family games
of Clue. No more arguing over who holds the popcorn bowl. No
more family outings to the beach or vacations to far-flung countries. No more family. After you told the therapist about the mis-
understandings and miscommunications and misdemeanors that
have brought you to this place, she asked: "Why did you stay?"
That question too took your breath away. "For my family," you say.

But this isn't an essay about the unraveling of a marriage. It's
an essay about knitting.

You realize now that all those years ago—fourteen, to be
exact—when you learned to knit, you knit things to comfort your

family, to warm them, to wrap them up. Long scarves and hats with pom-poms and misshapen wool socks. Your five-year-old daughter had died and that fall and winter you tried to knit your family back together. Of course back then you thought you were knitting so you wouldn't go crazy with grief. That was true too. You held on to those knitting needles for dear life, gripping them tight in your sweaty hands. Your teacher told you that there were only two stitches—knit and purl—and once you learned them you could knit anything. But like everything else you believed that wasn't exactly true. There was also knitting into the back of a stitch and slipping purlwise and slip slip knit and knit two together and so many more.

You believed too that on the unusually warm February morning when you got married to the Beatles' song "In My Life," clutching white tulips and celebrating with take-out Chinese food, that you were on your way to the rest of your happy life. You believed when you held your newborn daughter for the first time, her blue eyes already locked on you with a steady gaze, that you would hold her until the day you died. Instead you barely got to hold her at all. Five brief years. Instead, you are here, the tulips long gone, your daughter gone, pondering your next move. Where will you go? How will you move everything, a long marriage worth of stuff? You wish you didn't own so many books or so much yarn or so many beautiful platters. All of it hard to pack up. All of it seemingly impossible to dismantle.

So you knit. Small things. Things you can carry in your purse. Dishrags in colors of tropical birds. Coffee mug holders. Neck-warmers. Your needles fly. They do. Effortlessly, like you don't have a care in the world. When you knit you don't have to think about how your heart, that tough tender scarred muscle, aches. You don't cry when you knit. Or worry about ruining your children's lovely lives, the ones you've tended so carefully and with so much love that there have been times when you thought your heart, that same aching one, would burst with all that love. In an hour you have finished a dishrag, hot pink or lime green or shocking violet. You bind off the four stitches that are left, weave in the ends, fold it into a lopsided square and add it to your growing pile of other dishrags.

You decide to knit sixty dishrags before December 9, your sixtieth birthday. By then, you will have unpacked your things. You will have hung pictures on new walls. Made new bedrooms for your children. Acquired two cats and a Goldendoodle your daughter will name Coco. You decide to count off time with dishrags, the way you once marked time by counting the days without Grace. Here you are, impossibly, at five thousand one hundred and ten days without her. Here you are, with twenty-seven dishrags. On your anniversary, your husband used to take your wedding picture and recreate it in the material designated for that year: one year was cotton, two glass, three metal. He made stained glass and silkscreened and bent copper for you, counting the years you were together.

When you knit, you both think and don't think. You have to know how to increase at every row, the yarn over—*YO*—and then when you have forty stitches how to decrease, the knit two together, yarn over, knit two together—*K2TG YO K2TG*. A few months after Grace died, you decided to learn Italian. This was partially because the language you knew, the writing and reading you did, had done all your life, no longer made sense. But also because you needed to fill the Grace-less hours when you should have been singing in the car with her, marveling over her drawings, tucking her into bed. So you took a Beginners Italian book out of the library and stared at its pages: *Mi manchi. Aiuto! Quanto tempo!* But your brain was incapable of learning. Until the language of knitting, with its mysterious abbreviations and names of wool—fingerling, worsted, Aran—its vocabulary of stitches; its rules you struggle to understand.

Love has its own language too. The pet names that come early, when your given names aren't big enough to hold this huge new feeling. The looks that mean *Let's leave now, I want you, I adore you.* There is a vocabulary of silences too: the comfortable ones in the evening after dinner and wine, the breathless ones after lovemaking, the angry ones that lodge like rocks, finally, immovable.

But this is about knitting. It is not about grief. It is not about love. It is not about endings, endings that keep coming no matter how many blankets and scarves and sweaters and hats you knit, the yarn piling up, the stitches piling up, but none of it enough. Then why do it? Why pick up two needles and a skein of yarn again, cast on four or twenty or eleven stitches, and put one needle into a stitch and knit it? And keep knitting on and on until a cable snakes up the center or a seed stitch appears or a neat ribbing is ready to keep a hat from rolling up?

That fall and winter after Grace died, and even into the spring, I knit my way out of the crippling grief that had knocked me down. I knit a path with yarn, with hope, with *I love you* in every stitch. Will knitting sixty dishrags knit my way out of this new loss? All winter and spring I start another one, the vivid yarn, the number seven needles, the casting on of four stitches.

This is how love starts. A man dances you across your tiny living room to "Build Me Up, Buttercup." He gives you a ring with a sun and moon carved on the sides, a star sapphire at the center. He whispers, "The sun and the moon and the star, for you." It starts with a baby in your arms, six and half pounds, bald and blue eyed.

It starts when she says *Mama* for the first time, when she takes your face in her sticky hands and holds on tight.

Somehow you look up, and the man is angry and resentful, his back turned, his face turned, his eyes downcast. You are angry too, and turning away. Somehow you look up, and your daughter is saying *Mama* for the last time, she is on a gurney, she is gone.

It's evident, the poet Elizabeth Bishop tells you, "the art of losing's not too hard to master / though it may look like (*Write* it!) like disaster."

It may look like disaster, you think, staring out at the approaching summer. But you will look up again and there will be sixty dishrags, and your books in bookshelves, and a dog at your feet, and your children beside you, and soup on the stove. Cast on four stitches of chartreuse yarn. Knit those stitches. K2, YO, Knit to end of row. Repeat. Don't look up yet. Don't look up. Just knit.

contributors' notes

STEVE ALMOND is the author of eight books of fiction and non-fiction, most recently "Against Football." His work has appeared in *Best American Short Stories* and *Martha Stewart Living*. So there. Further information available here: againstfootball.org; Twitter: @stevealmondjoy.

ANNE BARTLETT has worked across a broad writing spectrum—magazines, children's education, oral history, biography, and fiction. She is best known for her novel *Knitting*, set in Adelaide, South Australia, and long-listed for the Miles Franklin Award. She is in the final stages of completing a novel titled *The Tiger Game*, but is often distracted by spinning and knitting. She holds a PhD in creative writing from the University of Adelaide, where she is currently an Honorary Research Fellow.

CYNTHIA CHINELLY is a poet and short story writer, whose work has appeared in numerous literary journals, including the *Montana Review*, *North Stone Review*, *Graham House Review*, the *Southern Poetry Review*, and *Mid-American Review*. She teaches writing at Florida International University.

MELISSA COLEMAN is the author of *This Life Is In Your Hands: One Dream, Sixty Acres, and a Family Undone*, a *New York Times* bestselling memoir about growing up during the 1970s back-to-the-land movement. Her writing has also appeared in publications including *The New York Times*, *O, The Oprah Magazine*, and *National Geographic Traveler*.

MICHAEL COLLIER is the author of six books of poetry, including *The Ledge*, which was a finalist for the National Book Critics Circle Award and the *Los Angeles Times* Book Prize. He has published a collection of essays about poetry and the writing life, *Make Us Wave Back*, and a translation of Euripides' *Medea*. He teaches at the University of Maryland and is the director of the Bread Loaf Writers' Conference.

STEPHANIE MANNATT DANLER is a writer living in Brooklyn. Her novel *Sweetbitter* was published by Knopf in 2016.

JARED FLOOD is a New York-based knitwear designer, yarn producer, and photographer. A Pacific Northwest native, Jared holds a BA from the University of Puget Sound and an MFA from the New York Academy of Art. His photography, knitwear design, and writings have been featured in several magazine, book, and online publications, including *Good Housekeeping*, *New York Spaces*, *New York Living*, *Vogue Knitting*, *Interweave Knits*, Random House, Potter Craft, Rodale, and Stewart, Tabori & Chang. In the fall of 2010 Jared launched his own line of artisanal, U.S.-made yarns. He currently spends his time working with his staff and design team at Brooklyn Tweed to produce original knitwear collections that support the company's domestic wool yarns. See more of his work at www.brooklyntweed.com.

NICK FLYNN's most recent book, *The Reenactments*, completes a trilogy begun with *Another Bullshit Night in Suck City* (2004). His previous book, *The Captain Asks for a Show of Hands* (2011), was a collection of poems linked to the second book of the trilogy, *The Ticking Is the Bomb* (2010). *Another Bullshit Night in Suck City* won the PEN/Martha Albrand Award, was short-listed for France's Prix Femina, and has been translated into fifteen languages. He is also the author of a play, *Alice Invents a Little Game and Alice Always Wins* (2008), as well as two other books of poetry, *Some Ether* (2000), and *Blind Huber* (2002), for which he received fellowships from, among other organizations, the Guggenheim Foundation and the Library of Congress. His film credits include artistic collaborator and "field poet" on the film *Darwin's Nightmare* (nominated for an Academy Award for best feature documentary in 2006), as well as executive producer and artistic collaborator on *Being Flynn*, the film version of *Another Bullshit Night in Suck City*. A professor in the creative writing program at the University of Houston, where he teaches each spring, he spends the rest of the year in (or near) Brooklyn.

DIANA GABALDON (pronounced "GAA-bull-dohn"—it rhymes with "bad to the bone") is the author of the award-winning, number one *New York Times*-bestselling *Outlander* novels, described by *Salon* magazine as "the smartest historical sci-fi adventure-romance story ever written by a science PhD with a background in scripting 'Scrooge McDuck' comics." A scientist with a PhD in quantitative behavioral ecology and a specialty in scientific computation, Gabaldon jumped the academic rails in 1991, when the adventure began with the classic *Outlander*, and has continued through seven more *New York Times*-bestselling novels, with 26 million copies in print worldwide, in forty countries and thirty-six languages. (Gabaldon has also written *The Exile*, an *Outlander* graphic novel, several novels of a subseries featuring Lord John Grey, and *The Scottish Prisoner*, featuring both Lord John and Jamie Fraser, as well as a number of novellas.) Starz has created a popular television series based on the books, also called *Outlander*——filmed in Scotland and presently sold in eighty-seven countries.

DEBRA GWARTNEY is the author of a memoir, *Live Through This*, a finalist for the National Book Critics Circle Award and Pacific Northwest Bookseller Award. Recent work has been published in *The Normal School*, *Prairie Schooner*, *The American Scholar*, and *Tin House*, and she was the 2013 winner of the *Crab Orchard Review* nonfiction prize. She teaches for the Pacific University MFA program in writing.

JANE HAMILTON has published six novels. Her short stories have appeared in *Harper's Magazine*. Her first novel, *The Book of Ruth*, won the PEN/Ernest Hemingway Foundation Award for best first novel and was a selection of Oprah's Book Club. Her second novel, *A Map of the World*, was an international bestseller. *The Short History of a Prince* was short-listed for the Orange Prize. *When Madeline Was Young* was on several Best of the Year lists. *Laura Rider's Masterpiece* was perhaps the book that made her laugh the most. She lives on a farm in Wisconsin.

CATHI HANAUER is the author of three novels, most recently *Gone*, and the editor of the number 10 *New York Times* bestselling essay anthology *The Bitch in the House*. A contributing writer at *Elle*, she also has written articles, essays, and/or reviews for *The New York Times*, *O, The Oprah Magazine*, *Real Simple*, *Self*, *Whole Living*, *Country Living*, and many other magazines. She was the monthly books columnist for both *Glamour* and *Mademoiselle* and wrote the monthly relationships advice column in *Seventeen* magazine for seven years. She lives in western Massachusetts with her husband, writer and editor Daniel Jones, and their kids. Find her at www.cathihanauer.com.

LILY KING is the author of four novels, the most recent of which, *Euphoria*, was the winner of the Kirkus Prize and the New England Book Award for Fiction, and named one of the *New York Times Book Review*'s 10 Best Books of the Year. She has been a novice knitter since the age of eight.

PERRI KLASS is a professor of journalism and pediatrics at New York University. She is the author of *Two Sweaters for My Father*, a collection of essays about knitting, and *Every Mother Is a Daughter: The Neverending Quest for Success, Inner Peace, and a Really Clean Kitchen (Recipes and Knitting Patterns Included)*, coauthored with her mother, Sheila Solomon Klass, along with many other works of fiction and nonfiction. She is the national medical director of Reach Out and Read, an early literacy program which works through pediatric primary care to encourage reading aloud to young children.

CHRISTINA BAKER KLINE is the author of five novels, including the number one *New York Times* bestselling *Orphan Train*, and has coauthored or edited five nonfiction books. Kline is the recipient of several Geraldine R. Dodge Foundation Fellowships and has received numerous other awards. She is currently working on a novel inspired by the Andrew Wyeth painting *Christina's World*.

ANN LEARY is the *New York Times* bestselling author of the novels *The Good House*, *Outtakes from a Marriage*, and the memoir *An Innocent, a Broad*. She has written for various magazines and anthologies. She lives on a small farm in northwestern Connecticut with several dogs, a few horses, and a husband.

CAROLINE LEAVITT is the *New York Times* bestselling author of *Is This Tomorrow* and *Pictures of You*, as well as seven other novels.

Pictures of You was a Costco Pennie's Pick, and a Best Book of the Year in the *San Francisco Chronicle*, *The Providence Journal*, *Bookmarks*, and one of the top five books from *Kirkus Reviews*. *Is This Tomorrow* was an Indie Next Pick, a *January* magazine Best Book of the Year, a *San Francisco Chronicle* Editor's Choice, a Jewish Book Council Pick, and the winner of an Audiophile Earphones Award. She is a book critic for *People*, *The Boston Globe*, and the *San Francisco Chronicle*, and she teaches novel writing online at Stanford and UCLA Writers' Program Extension and with private clients. Visit her at www.carolineleavitt.com.

LAURA LIPPMAN has won multiple prizes for her crime novels and short stories, which are published in more than twenty languages. She lives in Baltimore.

MAILE MELOY was named one of *Granta*'s Best Young American Novelists, and has received the PEN/Malamud Award and a Guggenheim Fellowship. Her stories have appeared in *The New Yorker* and *The Paris Review*, and she is the author of two novels, two story collections, and a young adult trilogy.

STEWART O'NAN is the author of fourteen novels, including *West of Sunset*, *Snow Angels*, *A Prayer for the Dying*, *Last Night at the Lobster*, and *Emily, Alone*. He was born and raised and lives with his family in Pittsburgh.

CLARA PARKES abandoned San Francisco's high-tech hubbub over a decade ago to build a quieter creative life on the coast of Maine. Since then, she has become a trusted voice in the knitting community. Named by *Vogue Knitting* as one of knitting's "New Wave" along with Debbie Stoller and Stephanie Pearl-McPhee,

Parkes is also the publisher of KnittersReview.com, has appeared regularly on the PBS television series *Knitting Daily TV*, and is a frequent contributor to *Twist Collective*. Her books include *The Knitter's Book of Socks*, *The Knitter's Book of Yarn*, *The Knitter's Book of Wool*, and *The Yarn Whisperer: My Unexpected Life in Knitting*.

JODI PICOULT is the author of twenty-three novels, including the number one *New York Times* bestsellers *Leaving Time*, *The Storyteller*, *Lone Wolf*, *Sing You Home*, *House Rules*, *Handle with Care*, *Change of Heart*, *Nineteen Minutes*, and *My Sister's Keeper*. She also cowrote the number one *New York Times* bestseller *Between the Lines*, the companion to *Off the Page*, with her daughter, Samantha van Leer. Several of her books have been made into television movies, and *My Sister's Keeper* was adapted for the big screen. Jodi lives in New Hampshire with her husband and three children. Visit her online at jodipicoult.com.

ROBIN ROMM is the author of a short story collection and a memoir, and the editor of the forthcoming anthology, *Double Bind: Women on Ambition*. Her memoir, *The Mercy Papers*, was a *New York Times* Notable Book of the Year, and a Best Book of the Year according to *Entertainment Weekly* and the *San Francisco Chronicle*. Her story collection, *The Mother Garden*, was a finalist for the PEN USA prize. She's written for *The New York Times*, *The Atlantic*, *Slate*, *Salon*, and *O, The Oprah Magazine*, and is a frequent contributor to *The New York Times Book Review*.

BILL ROORBACH is the author most recently of *The Remedy of Love*, which was a finalist for the 2014 Kirkus Fiction Prize. His novel *Life Among Giants*, a Maine Literary Award winner, is in development for a dramatic series with HBO. His memoir in nature, *Temple Stream*, also a Maine Literary Award winner, was just reissued by Down East Books in a new paperback. Most of Bill's knitting these days concerns his brows, but he still owns several items knitted during his college years, already forty years ago, Jesus. Find out more at www.billroorbach.com.

DANI SHAPIRO is the bestselling author of the memoirs *Devotion* and *Slow Motion*, and five novels including *Black & White* and *Family History*. Her work has appeared in *The New Yorker*, *Granta*, *Tin House*, *One Story*, *Elle*, *The New York Times Book Review*, the op-ed pages of *The New York Times*, the *Los Angeles Times*, and has been broadcast on *This American Life*. Dani was recently Oprah Winfrey's guest for an hour-long interview on *Super Soul Sunday*. She has taught in the writing programs at Columbia, NYU, The New School, and Wesleyan University, and is cofounder of the Sirenland Writers Conference in Positano, Italy. A contributing editor at *Condé Nast Traveler*, Dani lives with her family in Litchfield County, Connecticut. Her latest book is *Still Writing: The Pleasures and Perils of a Creative Life*.

SAMANTHA VAN LEER is a sophomore at Vassar College majoring in psychology with a minor in human development. She cowrote the number one *New York Times* bestseller *Between the Lines*, the companion to *Off the Page*, with her mother, Jodi Picoult.

LEE WOODRUFF is a journalist and the bestselling author of two memoirs, *In an Instant* and *Perfectly Imperfect*. Her first work of fiction, *Those We Love Most*, examines the complexities and secrets of families in the wake of trauma. She lives in Westchester County, New York, with her husband and four kids.

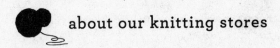

about our knitting stores

Churchmouse Yarns & Teas
118 Madrone Lane North
Bainbridge Island, WA 98110
(206) 780-2686
www.churchmouseyarns.com

When Kit Hutchin decided to open a yarn shop back in 1999, the name "Churchmouse" came to her almost instantly. Here's how it happened:

Kit worked as a professional writer for many years. Her assignments often included naming products and businesses. Eventually she was talked into taking a position as copy director to help Nordstrom launch their first-ever mail order catalog. It was a dream job. But after a few years, Kit realized that it just wasn't her dream. So she left to pursue her real calling, even though she didn't know what it was.

While she was considering what to do next, she found herself volunteering at her church. She spent so much time tiding up the lending library and teaching knitting classes that her husband fondly took to calling her "the Churchmouse."

One day, a friend said, why don't you just open a yarn store? She demurred, but her husband encouraged her to think about it. A week later, she said, "I'm going to open a yarn store. It will be called Churchmouse Yarns & Teas." Her husband said, "Churchmouse? Teas?" The name popped into her head right away and no other name was even considered. Kit's vision for her store was traditional and a bit English, and this name conveyed that well. When she created names for other businesses, there were usually months of work and many, many rounds of choices. For her business, the right name was always there from the beginning.

Churchmouse Yarns & Teas is a community shop on beautiful Bainbridge Island that's been providing a contemporary interpretation of the traditional fiber arts since 2000, as well as advocating for the satisfying pleasure of a decent cup of tea.

In 2010, Kit Hutchin and her team began publishing knitting and crochet patterns; today, Churchmouse designs can be found in hundreds of yarn shops around the world.

In 2012, Kit's team launched a website that's been called "churchmouseyarns dot calm." This site grows bit by digital bit every day.

Churchmouse prefers to be considered a "project shop" rather than a "yarn shop." Their customers come to find a project they can finish, enjoy making, and love wearing, not just more yarn to stash.

The "& Teas" part of the shop suggests all the beautiful ways you can add beauty and comfort to your crafting, such as knitting with a hearty cuppa poured from a traditional Brown Betty tea pot into a handmade English mug. And, some Scottish shortbread wouldn't go amiss.

Explore this shop on the island, or online at churchmouseyarns.com.

Hill Country Weavers

1701 South Congress Avenue
Austin, TX 78704
(512) 707-7396
www.hillcountryweavers.com

Why "Weavers"?

Our customers frequently ask why the store is called Hill Country Weavers—we're a yarn store. The answer is simple: things change.

Hill Country Weavers opened in 1981, in a space at 34th and Guadalupe. In addition to floor looms, weaving yarns, and classes, the store had a gallery that featured local weavers. In 1983, we moved to a larger location at Lamar and 12th. This space also had a gallery as well as more space for looms and yarn.

If you stepped into a way-back machine to see what kind of yarns were sold in 1981, you'd be very surprised. The store carried what was available: very traditional yarns for weaving—worsted spun wools and wool blends in solid colors. Although these yarns were on cones for weavers, knitters did find the store and started asking for needles, hooks, knitting patterns and classes. In the days before the Internet, we were Google for information on what was available in the knitting and fiber world. Customers came to Hill Country for what was new and trending in weaving and knitting.

In 1994 we moved to the current location on South Congress. Back then

South Congress was still a bit colorful. But the store became a cornerstone in the changing neighborhood. Today SoCo is a vibrant part of Austin, with its mix of residences, independently owned stores, and monthly street fetes featuring local artists and musicians.

If you visit the store, either in person or online, you'll feel our distinct Austin style—classic, eclectic, and a just little edgy. Our yarn inventory includes Woolfolk, Vice, Yarn Carnival, and Shelter, as well as Rowan, Shibui, and Habu. We are establishing new traditions with HCW-designed patterns that incorporate weaving with knitting and crochet. Our project kits take the stress out of choosing colors that work together. We encourage local designers with our pattern collections. Our challenge is to keep up with our customer's evolving demands for trending yarns and projects.

Today, we are first a yarn store. But if you peek into the classroom, you'll still see a loom or two.

Knit Purl
1101 Southwest Alder Street
Portland, OR 97205
(503) 227-2999
www.knit-purl.com

When Darcy Cameron founded Knit Purl in 2004, she wanted to create a unique curated experience for yarn buyers. Local, exclusive, and hard-to-find products became Knit Purl's wheelhouse, and eventually the store expanded to include both an online and brick-and-mortar presence.

Meanwhile, Darcy began her foray into pattern development and yarn sourcing, giving rise to Shibui, which eventually branched off into its own company.

Today, Knit Purl remains a source for exciting, modern, and one-of-a-kind knitting products, with its own exclusive yarns, patterns, and accessories. We have formed close personal bonds with local, regional, national, and international makers, designers, and buyers who expose us to their boundless creativity.

Our convenient downtown Portland location affords us the opportunity to connect with traveling knitters of all backgrounds and skill levels, and share their stories and experiences. We offer a variety of classes and workshops, and have an ongoing Knit Night that meets every other week most of the year.

Feel free to get in touch with us. We welcome your questions, and would love to see your current and finished objects.

Loop
1914 South Street
Philadelphia, PA 19146
(215) 893-9939
www.loopyarn.com

Crafting with yarn is a fantastic way to relax and be creative. With just a few basic stitches and techniques, you can knit and crochet anything from hats and socks, sweaters and scarves to blankets and afghans, pillows and toys. Whether for yourself or for others, it's rewarding to see your creations in use.

At Loop we want to help you experience your knitting and crocheting to the fullest. With beautiful materials, inspiring samples, and educational classes, our goal is to help you get the most from your knitting and crocheting.

Our online shop at loopyarn.com launched in October 2004. Our retail shop opened in its current location in April 2005. Thanks to you, we're approaching our tenth anniversary. We appreciate your business and your support, and look forward to serving you for many years to come.

Purl Soho
459 Broome Street
New York, NY 10013
(212) 420-8796
www.purlsoho.com

Purl opened in 2002 as a tiny yarn shop on Sullivan Street, in the heart of New York City's Soho neighborhood. Four years later and just a few doors down, we opened an even tinier store for fabric, Purl Patchwork. And in 2010 we finally realized our dream of bringing lovers of all needlecrafts together under one roof with the opening of our big, beautiful Purl Soho store. Sisters Joelle and Jennifer Hoverson and good friend Page Marchese Norman are the co-owners and visionaries behind Purl Soho. Editors and stylists in past lifetimes, we are bound together now by a passion for pure, natural fibers and exceptional design. We search the world over for the things we love—the timeless, the classic and the absolutely beautiful—in order to create a distinctive resource for fellow crafters who share our fervor.

From the very beginning, the true heart of our business has been our customers. At Purl Soho we have always worked to create a friendly, comfortable place for *everyone*: locals and tourists, beginners and old pros, regulars and onetime shoppers. We foster an environment where customers become friends and our place is yours. We love to answer questions, share accomplishments, research solutions, and exchange inspiration. It's why we do what we do!

We have also always maintained a vibrant online presence with our website, purlsoho.com and our blog, the Purl Bee (www.purlbee.com). We designed our purlsoho.com site to be as close to the experience of visiting our store as possible. Lovely, informative, and super user-friendly, purlsoho.com is your local yarn store at home! And the Purl Bee is our special depository for all the best ideas we have running through our heads. Chock-full of free patterns developed exclusively by our talented Purl Bee staff, crafters from all corners of the needlecraft world come here to find inspiration! In person or online, come visit! We'll be so happy to meet you!

The Yarnery
840 Grand Avenue #2
Saint Paul, MN 55105
(651) 222-5793
www.yarnery.com

The Yarnery has been a Minnesota fiber arts institution for more than forty years. Founded by the Kreisman family, the shop is now owned by Shelly Sheehan and Scott Rohr. Located on Grand Avenue in Saint Paul's most vibrant shopping district—historic Victoria Crossing—The Yarnery is surrounded by great restaurants and unique shops, with plenty of parking available.

Whether you shop at the store or online, you'll find high-quality natural fibers in a full range of weights and colors. The Yarnery is particularly proud of its exclusive relationships with some of the most in-demand yarn companies. The shop is a flagship stockist of Brooklyn Tweed, Woolfolk, and Neighborhood Fiber Co. yarns.

The shop also carries a comprehensive range of patterns from talented in-house and internationally known designers. After the publishing success of *Wearwithall: Knits for Your Life*, the Yarnery team recently launched a new pattern series; Wearwithall designs will feature modern classics for the entire family, from knitwear designers you love. Looking to learn? The Yarnery's class catalog is comprehensive and innovative, with teachers among the most respected in the industry.

At The Yarnery we take the needs of our customers seriously, even as we make knitting, weaving, and crocheting what it should be: fun! Count on finding the classes, clinics, and events that help you find the community you've been looking for. Please stop in and say hello; we'll help you find your perfect project.